The Lighthouse Method

How to Shine Again After You've Lost Your Light

By Angela C. Lalande

The Lighthouse Method:How to Shine Again After You've Lost Your Light

ISBN: 979-8-218-05171-6

Cover design by fingerplus

Edited by Hilary Jastram, www.bookmarkpub.com

DEDICATION

To the ones lost at sea–

Your story can be redeemed.

Shore is closer than you think.

TABLE OF CONTENTS

Foreword i

Introduction 1

Chapter 1 – The Light Inside You 13

Chapter 2 – Augustin Fresnel, the Maker of the Fresnel Lens 31

Chapter 3 – The Lighthouse Purpose and Method 43

Chapter 4 – Lost at Sea 67

Chapter 5 – Identifying a Person Lost at Sea 83

Chapter 6 – Found at Sea 97

Chapter 7 – Becoming a Prism 113

Chapter 8 – Pierce the Night 141

Acknowledgments 157

About the Author 159

"The rocky ledge runs far into the sea,
and on its outer point, some miles away....
A pillar of fire by night, of cloud by day."

—Henry Wadsworth Longfellow

FOREWORD

I have had the pleasure of knowing Angela Lalande for a few years. One thing you know about Angela—whether you have known her for a day or a decade—is that she has a fire about her and a drive that has pushed her from failure, seeming defeat, challenges, setbacks, mistakes, and struggle. Some people will let life's challenges be an excuse to throw in the towel or settle for less, but not Angela. She has used every one of these as fuel. Instead of burning her out, they only made her flame burn brighter.

Angela is a wife, a mom, an entrepreneur, an attorney, and a writer. She is an inspiration to many women with a big heart, big vision, and big dreams. I have mentored many women who may have big dreams, yet they never see them through to fruition. What sets Angela apart is following through. She doesn't just talk the talk, but she walks the walk. If it is in her heart to do it, she will do what it takes to get the job done.

Humility is rare in such individuals. Angela is seasoned with grace and humility, fully aware of her dependence on God and the ability He has placed inside her. The beautiful thing is that the people that God can use at the greatest capacity are those who stay humble. I think of Moses in the Bible, able to be used by God in the greatest measure because his heart was humble before God and others. I admire Angela's grace and humility, and after all that she has achieved, she is kind, approachable, and always looking for someone to be a blessing to.

I am so excited for her to get this book out! Angela is an exceptional and vulnerable writer. In "The Lighthouse Method," you will encounter a raw transparency that will meet you right where you are—in your darkest hour with words that ring true to your heart. It will meet you in your own brokenness and shame as if she has been a fly on the wall of your valley. I believe this book will be the lighthouse you are searching for in the middle of your storm. I am thankful that Angela is using her story to shine a light for you—a light of hope. I know she has prayerfully considered every word, and I know she has prayed for you, the reader. Get ready to be strengthened and encouraged. It's a good one!

—Alicia Hankins Moran

INTRODUCTION

"Take notice of what light does—to everything."

—Tess Guinery

Lost.

That's where I was eleven years ago, after having just graduated from law school.

Broken, cast away, flailing my arms aimlessly under the waters of failure, rejection, and sadness, with the heaviness stemming from choices I had made tormenting me. Looking back, I see that I flailed for a long time without the full resolve to go upward because somewhere in the back of my mind, I believed I deserved to sink.

One would think I would have been on my way to embarking on an incredible personal and professional journey, but due to trust I had broken and betrayals I had caused, I wasn't on that path.

No, my path was not one of light.

It was much darker.

In fact, I was on the darkest path of my life.

I had been rejected from becoming an attorney due to an honor code violation in law school—

Plagiarism.

It's still a word that is hard to say or type. A word that has scarred me. A word I never thought I would be associated with.

Writing—my greatest gifting—the very thing that brought me immense joy prior to this time, had now brought me nearly debilitating pain.

On top of that, I was living a lie of being a happy, faithful wife.

I was parading around with a mask over my life and a scarlet "A" branded on my chest.

Adultery.

It's also a word I never thought I would invite into my life.

I had become someone I didn't know.

I had become someone I didn't want to know.

During these darkest days, I could not see the light to end my night of wondering what my next professional step would be or if I had a marriage after being unfaithful.

I was fearful I had condemned myself to live in the shadows for the rest of my life.

I was afraid of what I had turned myself into and feared that I had done such a great job of messing up my life that there was no way out.

Was I this person I had come to hate?

Was that really who I would always have to be?

Would my failures be all others would remember me for?

Was I the warden *and* the prisoner—denying myself the keys to redemption?

Would I let the devil have the last say?

My existence was so dark that I couldn't see anything good about me—my light, the light that shines for myself and others. I certainly could not have fathomed the thought of being a light for anyone else. I was in such blinding pain.

Rain steadily pitter-pattered on my heart.

What would my future hold?

Would the waves of shame overcome me?

Would I ever find Harbor?

In case you're wondering why I chose to capitalize this word, let me give you a little peek into The Lighthouse Method. Step 5—the very last step—in The Lighthouse Method is *Find Harbor and Become It*. This step is the final release from your pain and the redemption from unforgiveness.

Don't worry; I will explain this method in greater detail in these pages. If I can follow these steps and unchain myself, you can, too.

My favorite part is that regardless of what you have done or wrought in your life, you will learn that you are still worthy.

Yes, you are worthy.

Even as you are sitting here in your own darkness dredging up your worst sins, God only sees you as a child to be loved. In His eyes, you are already redeemed, and He wants to take you on a journey of healing and redemption so you will see yourself that way too.

Through my experience and the birth of The Lighthouse Method and its five steps, I am going to teach you how to get there. Yes, we will talk about accepting what you have done or had done to you—because sometimes, we are plunged into darkness through outside circumstances—but the greatest part of what you are about to learn is how to love yourself again.

But not just now.

You will learn how to love yourself *always*.

RISING UP

As the author of this message, you know I did not sink to the bottom of the ocean, never to be seen again. Indeed, I found my way back to the surface.

I became an overcomer, a survivor, and a champion.

But the swim to rise up and survive created scars. Some more hideous than others. Some deeper than others.

And that's okay.

They are merely reminders of where I've been, who I thought I was during my lost season, and who I know I am now.

THE ONES

The words I speak through this book are for *the ones—the ones* who, like I once was, are lost.

The ones who may be sinking or *the ones* who may be walking toward the ledge of the very quicksand that could negatively change the course of their life forever.

The ones who have disqualified themselves after a monumental failure.

The ones seeking to be pulled out of the waves of depression that come from their decisions or life circumstances.

Initially, this book started as a letter. I even named it *A Letter for the One.*

Imagine that.

And as the script has grown from a letter to a book, so, too, have the people who were destined to read it. It's not just for *the one.*

It is for *the ones…* lost at sea.

As the *Dedication* to this book succinctly states.

I believe writing that letter was a divine prompting from God.

Because I felt the prompting to share its contents with others, as you will soon read within these pages.

Others who would learn about my past.

Others who would not just see my scars but learn how I got them.

I could see myself speaking in front of law school students or prospective students, sharing the importance of honor in their personal and professional lives.

Telling them of the value in seeing life through the proper lens—one that is clear, not muddied by mistakes that will make their lens very difficult to wipe clean.

To make choices that wouldn't jeopardize their future as members of the legal community.

As I was speaking, I could see that my testimony was rescuing some of the students from having to experience the pain from the aftermath of an incident like mine.

Some had not yet crossed the boundary.

But some already had.

Those students were either crying inside—frowning, fiddling with their shoelaces—or frozen because they saw I was them.

And somehow, my words could penetrate and rescue them too.

Because they knew there was hope

Even in what may seem like the darkest season of their life.

I knew the compulsion to write *A Letter for the One* was from God because I know me.

I like to write the script—I don't like being on stage giving the message.

That doesn't matter. God has His plans, and I am determined to follow what He has written for me.

The letter stayed on my laptop for a year before it developed into the book it is now.

It wasn't until I was jotting down notes for the chapter I authored in the *USA Today* Bestselling book, *The Younger Self Letters*, that the image of a lighthouse dropped into my spirit.

I remember the moment vividly and knew immediately it was for this book.

THE LIGHTHOUSE METHOD IS BORN

I was sitting on my bed typing out sparks of creative light that made their way into my mind and then flowed out of my fingers, through the keyboard, and onto the screen.

That's the beauty of inspiration. You never know when it will strike. When it does, you better be ready.

I took a break from writing and began researching lighthouses.

I continued to see the name "Augustin Fresnel" during my search. I had no idea who he was but thought he must be important.

I read that he was a French physicist whose invention of what has come to be known as the Fresnel Lens revolutionized lighthouse technology in the early 19th century.

A Fresnel Lens consists of several concentric sections of cut glass or prisms that can take all the light emanating from a light source and channel it in the same direction. This permits the light in a lighthouse to intensify and bend in such a way that it can penetrate the night over 20 miles out to sea.

Before Fresnel's invention, too many sailors were lost to shipwrecks. Because the light emitted from lighthouses was not bright enough, ships would run aground or wreck on the rocks because they could not see where they were.

Fresnel saved millions of lives with his invention and made a way for light in a lighthouse to pierce the night.

YOUR LIGHT

Did you know your light can pierce the night, too?

Yes, oh yes.

It can.

You carry this light inside you.

But it was never meant to be contained there.

Much like the light inside a lighthouse—your light's purpose goes beyond the exterior of the shell that holds it. Your light is a piece of Heaven inside you. This divine radiance has the ability to illuminate hidden corners of the human heart and heal dark places.

When you shine your light, people unmistakably know where it's coming from. Have you ever read a social media post and knew who wrote it before you looked at it? Your light is your spirit's DNA.

It shines the brightest when we share it with others—and when we accept the light that others want to share with us.

We are brighter together.

Our light is transformative.

It was made to pierce the night.

In her book, "A Return to Love: Reflections on the Principles of a Course in Miracles," Marianne Williamson said, "We are all meant to shine, as children do. We were born to make manifest the glory of God that is within us. It's not just in some of us; it's in everyone. And as we let our own light shine, we unconsciously give other people permission to do the same."

She is right.

You were made to shine, and I am going to show you how you can again.

When I was lost at sea, this is where I discovered the principles of The Lighthouse Method. Applying these principles to my life saved me, empowered me, allowed me to shine my brightest once again, and now I can lead others to do the same.

In this book and through The Lighthouse Method, you will learn to:

- Prepare to Rise Up
- Become a Prism
- Have the Right Support System
- Bend Your Light and Shine
- Find Harbor and Become It

You *Prepare to Rise Up* by casting the vision for healing, committing to taking regular actions to stay healthy, honoring your emotions, fighting to reclaim your life, and borrowing another's light if you absolutely cannot find your own.

You *Become a Prism* by being transparent and purified, where the impurities in your life are extracted. This allows light to pass through you and out into the world around you.

When you *Have the Right Support System*, your light can pierce the night. Just as a light in a lighthouse cannot shine without proper support, you cannot shine without the right people around you or the Holy Spirit inside of you to give you the ability to shine like you have the potential to do.

You *Bend Your Light and Shine* when you change direction. As light passes through a lens in a lighthouse, the light bends, and the light rays unify in the same direction. This is known as refraction. After you become a prism and light can pass through you, your light will change direction! You will change direction.

When you *Find Harbor and Become It*, you will rise up out of the waters of depression, anxiety, and fear and courageously take your steps to reach the shore. Once there, you will turn around and plant your feet in the sand. With eyes roaming the horizon, you will know it is your turn to rescue another lost mariner and bring them home.

THIS BOOK IS FOR YOU

This book will help you move from the darkness of depression, tragedy, or strife to light. It is designed to help you shine your brightest even when all hope of finding your light is gone.

If you feel lost or invisible, this book is for you. You will recapture the joy in who you are by learning to reject the voices in your head dragging you down.

If you are feeling shame and fear, this book is for you. You will learn to forgive yourself and others for those weaker moments in life when you may lose control or suffer extreme hurt.

If you feel broken beyond repair, this book is for you. No matter how you got this way, you will learn to reframe your life into one that you want to live. You will learn to fight for yourself and care about what happens to you.

If you have been betrayed at the deepest level that takes your breath away, this book is for you. Now, you can count down the days when you won't feel sucker-punched when you wake up. You will realize a new life is waiting for you, and you will be eager to go and get it.

If you have disqualified yourself after a monumental failure and seek to be pulled out of the waves of depression, this book is for you. We all fall down, and within these pages, you will find the strength to get back up.

Learn the principles of The Lighthouse Method and apply its steps to your life so you, too, will be saved.

You will learn to shine again.

And your light will give others permission to move out of their darkness.

Your light *will* pierce the night!

CHAPTER 1

THE LIGHT INSIDE YOU

"God uses broken things.
It takes broken soil to produce a crop, broken clouds to give rain,
broken grain to give bread, broken bread to give strength.
It is the broken alabaster box that gives forth perfume.
It is Peter, weeping bitterly, who returns to greater power than ever."

—Vance Havner

Ernest Hemingway said, "We are all broken—that's how the light gets in." I'd like to propose that the opposite is true. In many cases, brokenness brings an opportunity for our light to shine through the cracks—in the places and spaces inside of us that appear to be crumbling from trauma caused by our choices or the choices of others.

Brokenness has been defined as "a state of strong emotional pain that stops someone from living a normal or healthy life."[1]

The progressive and consistent wounding of a person's soul without healing leads to brokenness.

---

[1] https://dictionary.cambridge.org/us/dictionary/english/brokenness

You could be walking around with soul wounds caused by any of the following:

Rejection   From people or communities you desire to be a part of

Abandonment   Of a relationship or a child (whether you were the child abandoned or you abandoned a child)

Unforgiveness   A hardened heart toward yourself or another person; lacking love

I have carried wounds from all these things. I have rejected what I knew in my heart to do—and thankfully, I learned to live a different way. If I hadn't, I would be a fragment of myself, and if you continue down the wrong path, I hate to tell you, but that is your destiny, too.

Before we dive into how we can love ourselves as broken, let me speak about rejection for a moment.

REJECTION

No one likes being rejected, whether it's not being picked to be on a team or having that boy or girl you like not like you back. In this same vein, I ask you not to reject me here and now. In this book, I am going to share my heart with you. You will see my failures, trials, and tribulations. You will also see redemption. I will share with you my faith and how God redeemed my story. You will see many scripture references from the Bible throughout this book because I believe the Bible to be the ultimate source of knowledge.

Reverend Billy Graham once said, "While people today–from all walks of life–are searching for answers to life's problems, only the Bible has the answer to the deepest needs of men, women, and children."[2]

I believe this.

I believe scripture to be God-breathed. I believe scripture can heal. I believe scripture can transform hearts and minds. There is power in God's Word.

You may come from a different religious or spiritual background, or you may come from none at all. Please don't push me away because we may be different in our beliefs. I love you, and my heart's desire is for you to be healed and love yourself again.

On one of my darkest days, I was rejected from becoming an attorney.

You will read about it in the coming pages.

I made a horrible mistake when I was in law school, and it almost stopped me from fulfilling my life's call, forever changing the course of my life.

Plagiarism.

There, I said it again. It's still difficult to roll the word off my tongue or pen.

The very area I have been gifted in—writing—became the very area that brought me to one of the deepest pains of my life.

In the aftermath of this incident, the legal community rejected me.

I rejected me.

---

[2] https://www.elizabethton.com/2021/10/05/the-bible-is-the-source-of-all-knowledge/

On this day, a little over eleven years ago, I felt broken beyond repair. I had just moved home to Louisiana, separated from my husband at that time.

I was living in my parent's house—in the room I grew up in as a child. This was the room I shared with my twin sister, Kathryn. The walls were painted a pale green—they matched the hue of my heart during this time.

I felt like I was fading.

I had just spent the last month preparing for the Mississippi Bar Exam—the prestigious test one takes that allows them, when they pass, to become an attorney who is licensed to practice law. I had spent nearly twenty years of school to get me to this moment in time.

With the average lifespan of a person being 73.2 years[3], I had spent over a quarter of my life preparing to get to this point.

And in an instant, it was gone.

I had self-sabotaged any progress I made by being dishonest about my work. If you know me, I was just as surprised as you. I had never in my life ever done anything even remotely close to what I did. I let down my professor, parents, friends, relatives, and most importantly myself. It has taken me a long time to write about it with such transparency but doing so is why I have been able to heal.

Are you hiding from something you have done or a situation in your life you're ashamed of?

I can't adequately describe how freeing it is to tell my story now.

As the years have gone by, I can see why I made the decision I did. More importantly, I am so grateful that I chose to love myself despite it.

---

[3] https://www.worldometers.info/demographics/life-expectancy/

I was sitting at a desk in my childhood bedroom, buried in bar exam studies, when I learned that as a result of my poor decision, I would not be allowed to sit for the Mississippi Bar Exam. This was the biggest test of my life to date.

I didn't want anyone to know about the massive failure I had made of myself—particularly my parents. My shortcomings were almost too much to bear.

All I knew to do, and all I desired to do, was numb the pain. I wanted to drown out the sound of rejection that was resounding in my spirit.

So, what did I do? I found the closest store that would sell me a bottle of vodka, and I drove around my hometown with the intention to saturate myself in it until my sadness left.

How could I let the world down like this?

How could I let myself down like this?

How could I move on?

These were all questions I asked myself. Questions I didn't know quite how to answer. All I knew was that hiding was not an option.

But I would do it until the bottle ran out.

That didn't happen, but I had the best of intentions to drink that bottle dry. I drove my car to a prominent neighborhood in town located not far from the neighborhood I grew up in. Driving slowly down the streets, I marinated in my intense feelings of rejection and sadness. I'm sure I looked somewhat suspicious, idling in front of random houses with my left hand on the steering wheel and my right hand wrapped around a bottle of Tito's.

But no one called the cops.

I was still in prison, though.

This is a painful moment that marked me.

It was a moment where I chose to harbor unforgiveness instead of healing. It was a time when I had completely lost my identity, and I felt like my innermost being had been shattered into a million pieces.

I was broken.

Something tells me you can relate.

The good news is I didn't stay that way, and I want to reassure you that you don't have to, either.

I made a choice to rise again.

I made a choice to move forward.

I became purified so the light within me could shine.

I became refined by fire, and the impurities within me melted away.

Purified, redeemed—so the light within me could shine.

I found Harbor.

If you've come here broken, know that your story can be redeemed.

You can rise again.

Now is the time for you to let your light shine through your cracks.

Now is the time for you to push through your darkness.

MY CONNECTION TO LIGHTHOUSES

I have always been drawn to lighthouses. Visually because of their beauty but even more so because of what they represent symbolically–a tower, a beacon, a shining light to those lost at sea. They are a searchlight to show one where to go, and they can illuminate the way for one who has fallen off course or who may not even know they have drifted toward the rocks.

Lighthouses are unwavering, standing tall in the confidence that darkness cannot overcome them simply because they exist. They seem to know that even though the night is coming, the ones who feel lost will always be found by the light they carry.

I only recently visited one for the first time. I don't know why I waited so long, but better late than never, I guess.

My husband and I were returning from a weekend getaway to The Woodlands, Texas, with my twin sister and her husband when we decided to tour Lake Conroe, a 22,000-acre lake located just north of Houston. I had no idea we would see a lighthouse that day. The thought of cruising around a well-known lake in the area is what captured us to begin with.

We found a local breakfast eatery in Conroe. The pancakes were sensational. I do not remember the name of the restaurant, but I do remember the excellent manners of our server! He was so polite, and I thought, *His parents have raised him well.* He asked us what we were in town for— which was truthfully breakfast and sightseeing around Lake Conroe. He suggested we go to Waterpoint Marina. You could charter a boat and tour the lake. That sounded perfect, so we decided that was our next stop. After inhaling eggs, pancakes, and coffee, we drove down the road a bit and found the marina.

It was the end of July in Texas—and hot! I could feel the sweat on my brow. When we arrived at the marina, we got out of the car and walked toward the boardwalk.

While a boat tour sounded inviting, we thought about the heat and the fact that we had three tiny humans at home waiting for us to return. Ultimately, we opted for a self-guided drive around the lake. As we looked around and saw boats lining the marina, we thought the place was cute.

Then I spotted a map that could give us directions on where to go around this lake. The first thing I saw on the map was a picture of a lighthouse.

My face lit up when I saw it.

I even think the name of the attraction point was "The Lighthouse." I could barely believe it! Seeing those words further confirmed that I had to write this book on the parallel of lighthouses and how brightly we can shine just like them—no matter the darkness we may feel inside.

I also knew that seeing the picture of a lighthouse was not enough for me— I had to see it up close!

We hopped in our car and made our way to the lighthouse. While we didn't know the exact location, we had a general idea of where it was from the picture on the map.

As it turns out, it wasn't as easy to find as one might imagine. As we drove through one of the neighborhoods, a man was outside playing with his son. We told him why we were in the area, and he offered to lead us to the lighthouse in his golf cart.

I'm glad he showed us the way because we were going in the wrong direction!

He took us to Harbour Town, the neighborhood where the lighthouse was. We knew we were at the right place because two large model lighthouses stood at the entrance to the neighborhood. The man pointed out which way to go to reach it. We thanked him and drove to where he pointed.

And then we saw a gate.

Uh oh. We must need a code to get in.

None of us knew what it was.

We did, however, have the grit and determination to get inside that gate!

We turned our car around and waited for another vehicle to drive up to the gate—whose driver *did* have the code. When that car arrived, we all smiled excitedly because we knew we were almost inside. The driver of the car saw us too and likely knew what we were attempting. He punched the code on the padlock, then drove in, and so did we! A woman in her yard just inside the gate noticed us, too, and said something I couldn't hear, but she pointed back at the gate with a frown.

We knew we were not welcome.

Still, we kept driving.

We just *had* to get to the lighthouse!

Please know I am not advocating entering gated communities without permission. We should have had permission to go inside the gate.

We began making our way to the lakeside properties, knowing we would find it eventually. My heart was beating fast. I looked back to make sure the woman wasn't following us. I could imagine her running down the road, shaking her fist or gardening tools in the air.

Thankfully, she was nowhere to be found.

I got more excited. With each passing second, we were closer to the lighthouse. Suddenly, as we rounded a corner, we saw it standing in the sun.

The Lake Conroe Lighthouse is a 90-foot octagonal, cylindrical tower painted with alternating red and white bands, a copper top, steel frame, and stucco siding, built to look like Harbour Town Lighthouse in Hilton Head, South Carolina. This iconic landmark is located on a point jutting into the east side of Lake Conroe. Originally built in 1977 to aid in navigation, this lighthouse was badly damaged by a tornado in 1999 and subsequently rebuilt.

We parked our car on the side of the road beside an open lot and made our way to the strip of land leading up to the lighthouse. To our right was a marina filled with boats. Water gently lapped against the boats as we passed. To our left was a building that looked like a house. Through the windows, you could see several round tables in the middle of an open room. It looked like an event hall, but I imagined it may have been someone's home at one time.

Being there was almost surreal. What a gift to share this moment with my husband. I doubt he was as giddy inside as I was to be there, but I also know one of his deepest desires is to make me happy, and he was.

As I gazed at the lighthouse, my eyes traveled straight to the top, where I saw a giant lens that appeared to be encased by windows. This is where light is produced to shine out over the open water.

Immediately, it struck me that just as there is light inside a lighthouse, we also have light inside us.

We continued to walk closer to the lighthouse, and my mind drifted back to my childhood— as a child, I collected lighthouse calendars. Whenever

I saw a lighthouse in a picture, I could feel my spirit rise. There was a knowing deep inside me of the battle between light and dark.

Early on in my life, the image of the lighthouse gave me hope that light would always prevail. And it does.

---

2 Corinthians 4:6 says, "For God, who said, 'Let light shine out of darkness,' made his light shine in our hearts to give us the light of the knowledge of God's glory displayed in the face of Christ."

Light will always shine out of darkness.

I know this to be true.

WHAT IS LIGHT?

Did you know the word "light" is used 272 times in the Bible?[4] It must be dear to God, based on its use in scripture! Light has been associated with God's revelation, holiness, wisdom, grace, and hope. By contrast, darkness has been associated with sin, evil, and oppression.

What else do we know about light other than it being the opposite of dark? I always turn to the dictionary to peel away a word's layers so I can better understand what it means.

Oxford Languages defines light as "the natural agent that stimulates sight and makes things visible."[5]

I want to break this down for you because understanding light and how it relates to you paves the way for the rest of this book.

---

[4] https://www.jesusbelieverjd.com/bible-verses-about-light-in-the-new-testament-kjv/
[5] https://www.google.com/search?q=light+definition

LIGHT MAKES THINGS VISIBLE.

Without light, you cannot see.

Let that sink in for a moment.

I'm not talking about a physical light in a room. I am talking about the deeper things—the intangibles.

Without light, you can't see the people in front of you who are reaching out to you in your darkness.

People who love you.

Without light, you cannot see where you are supposed to go because your path is not visible.

Without light, you are blinded to the truth about situations and circumstances in your life because you cannot see with clarity.

But with light, *with* light!

Your darkness is illuminated.

Psalm 18:28 says, "For You light my lamp; The LORD my God illumines my darkness."

Light gives us the ability to see in the dark. With light, we not only see the hands of our loved ones reaching out to us; we can take hold of them!

Light removes our fear of moving forward because we can see where we are going.

LIGHT IS A NATURAL AGENT

It's interesting how light is described as a "natural agent." The word "natural," when used as an adjective, means "existing in or caused by nature; not made or caused by humankind."[6]

Genesis 1:1-4 says, "In the beginning God created the heaven and the earth. And the earth was without form, and void; and darkness was upon the face of the deep. And the spirit of God moved upon the face of the waters. And God said, 'Let there be light,' and there was light. And God saw the light, and it was good; and God divided the light from the darkness."

In other words, light is an existing matter—something found in the earth and not made by the hands of man—but created by God.

"Agent" is defined as "a thing that takes an active role or produces a specified effect."[7] As it relates to light, the specified effect is to make objects and entities visible.

Ephesians 5:13 tells us, "But all things become visible when they are exposed by the light, for everything that becomes visible is light."

Our light is internal and overflows to the external. It may not have a color, but it is still visible to others and can bring visibility to others. We may not be able to touch it, but from a spiritual perspective, it can be seen.

Every one of our lights allows people to see with an eternal perspective.

---

[6] https://dictionaryofdefinitions.blogspot.com/2016/02/what-is-meaning-definition-of-natural.html.

[7] https://www.lexico.com/en/definition/agent

LIGHT STIMULATES SIGHT

To stimulate means to "encourage development of or increased activity in (a state or process)."[8] When something is stimulated, an igniting occurs, then a transference of energy builds upon itself progressively, which causes a noticeable increase of activity in a state or process.

By definition, light encourages the development or increased activity in sight.

And don't you want to be able to see?

Light is an instrumental part of The Lighthouse Method, and you must know you have it—you must take hold of it and let it shine out of you if you want to move forward.

The point I want to drive home to you is that darkness cannot overcome you because of the light inside you. You may feel like your light has gone out, but it is there. With this light, you will be able to see again. You will be able to move out of your darkness.

**Ultimately, your light will give others
permission to move out of their darkness.**

What you are about to read will finally release you from the darkness of depression, anxiety, and fear. You will remember that even if you are living in a night season, light is on the inside waiting to break out. You will learn how to shine again.

DON'T TURN THE PAGE YET

Before we move on, close your eyes, and take a deep breath.

---

[8] https://www.lexico.com/en/definition/stimulate

We're about to dive deep into memories you hoped would never rise to the surface of your mind again.

Don't be scared. Your fear only stands on the brink of your healing. It cannot come with you when you take that step to be free from the darkness of depression, anxiety, and fear that is trying to hold you captive.

When you inhale, I want you to ponder this question: *What happened in your life to make you feel like you have no light to shine?*

As you exhale, visualize your wall coming down. You know, the one you made. The wall you put up in an attempt to guard yourself against the pain of shame, blame, regret, betrayal, or unforgiveness. With this wall raised, you can't truly examine or confront the incidents in your life. You will not be able to heal properly.

Have you broken trust?

Has your trust been broken?

Have you abandoned a relationship?

Have you been abandoned by someone you love?

Are you refusing to love others?

Are you refusing to love yourself?

Your wall must come down! Either tear it down or remain in prison— your choice.

I suspect that if you've picked up this book, you're ready to be free. So come to these pages with an open mind. Be vulnerable when you search your heart and know that saying yes is a step toward the light—the place you so desperately desire to be.

Now relax and open your eyes and heart.

WE ARE VESSELS

Our light was never designed to be contained inside. Much like the light inside a lighthouse—our light's purpose goes beyond the exterior of the shell that holds it.

And this light, well, this is your light, and it is transformative.

It was made to pierce the night.

You were made to see.

You were made to be seen.

You were made to rise.

This light inside you brings victory.

It tramples over fear. It takes you out of the dark so you can see yourself and the world through the proper lens.

The catch is the light is on the inside—of you.

Not the outside where you are huddled in a cell.

You won't find it there.

So let it out!

I know you're tired of sitting in the shadows.

But how in the world do you get out?

Come a little closer and let me tell you all about The Lighthouse Method.

WHY THE LIGHTHOUSE METHOD?

If you are like me—and probably the majority of the population--you may need actionable steps to take to rise and shine again after being submerged in the darkness of depression following a traumatic experience. Otherwise, the mere thought of standing up out of the darkness can seem overwhelming. Some people are so lost and so far under that they don't know where to begin. They don't know how in the world the light will reach them and, in turn, how their light can reach others.

This is the beauty of The Lighthouse Method, a system that walks you through the steps to unleash the light inside you. It will allow your light to pierce the night so you can shine once again. With this method, you no longer have to ask yourself, "*What's my first step?*" because it is laid out for you here.

The Lighthouse Method can be used again and again to help you rise up out of tragedy, strife, and devastation. Life is unpredictable, and you never know when you may need to turn toward these resources. So, remember to reach for this book on your darkest days.

While the steps of The Lighthouse Method are designed to help you see and turn on the light that has diminished by your own hand because of choices you have made, they also can be used if you're looking to shine once again—regardless of how you landed in your darkness. In the coming pages, I will teach you everything you need to know to shine again using these steps.

Follow them, and you will shine your brightest even when all hope of ever finding your light is gone. You will also be more resilient for the next challenge, which means you are better positioned to thrive.

HOW DO I KNOW?

When I finally followed the path I am about to teach you, my light eclipsed the darkness. Honestly, I took too long to take these steps. I wish someone had told me about what you are about to read in the way you are about to read it. Maybe it could have saved me some heartache. That said, I am here now, and I want you to have the opportunity to shine *now*. But before I teach you the steps you need to know, let me introduce you to the man who paved the way for the creation of The Lighthouse Method.

CHAPTER 2

AUGUSTIN FRESNEL,
THE MAKER OF THE FRESNEL LENS

"Into my heart's night along a narrow way I groped; and lo!
The light, an infinite land of day."

—Rumi

In preparing to write this book, I had a tremendous amount of help from an incredible book: *A Short Bright Flash: Augustin Fresnel and the Birth of the Modern Lighthouse.* Let me pay homage to Theresa Levitt, who taught me so much about lighthouses and Augustin Fresnel; this book and other readings made the writing of this book possible!

FROM SHIPWRECKS TO FRESNEL

For sailors in the early 19th century, a shipwreck meant almost certain imminent death. One of the most notable shipwrecks during this time was the tragic wreck of the French frigate *La Meduse*, which had run aground off the west coast of Africa on July 2, 1816. Over 150 people were forced to take refuge on a makeshift twenty by sixty-foot raft made of broken masts and planks while lifeboats towed it with a rope. However, it didn't take very long before the lifeboats abandoned the raft and its passengers, leaving them with little hope of survival. Many were washed away by inclement weather, thrown into the sea, or killed by officers. Some passengers even resorted to cannibalism to stay alive. After spending 13 days at sea, the raft was found. Only 15 of the more than 150 people originally on it were alive.[9]

This is only one story of the many that can be told of lives lost when they should not have been.

The questions remain, If the crew on the ship could have seen how close they were to shore, would they have run aground? If there was a light bright enough to allow them to see through the night or fog, would they have been saved?

I believe if a lighthouse had been on shore with a Fresnel Lens inside, these sailors would have been saved.

THE INVENTOR OF THE FRESNEL LENS

Augustin Jean Fresnel was a shy architect who had been commissioned to build roads and bridges in remote corners of France. But that's not what he is most remembered for. The world knows him as the French physicist whose invention of the Fresnel Lens revolutionized lighthouse technology. It has been called "the invention that saved a million ships."[10]

> Fresnel was known to be quiet and small for his age and always in rather precarious health. He was also slow, lagging behind his brothers in their school lessons. While he may have been perceived as behind in education as a child, he was also regarded as a genius by his friends due to the number of experiments he performed on make-shift artillery he and his friends made for their playful neighborhood battles.

---

[9] https://en.wikipedia.org/wiki/French_frigate_M%C3%A9duse_(1810)
[10] https://en.wikipedia.org/wiki/Fresnel_lens.

When he was 13, Fresnel attended a central school in Caen, France, with his older brother, Louis. Their other brother, Leonor, joined them the following year, and the three brothers flourished. In 1804, the brothers attended Ecole Polytechnique, a school known for bringing France's top scientific minds together and providing the world's most rigorous, up-to-date education. After graduating in 1806, Fresnel continued his studies at the National School of Bridges and Highways, the world's oldest school of civil engineering, where he graduated in 1809 with the title of ingenieur ordinaire aspirant (translated to mean "an ordinary engineer in training").

Fresnel's first assignment was to the Vendee region of France, where he was commissioned to connect a new town built on the river Yon to serve as a military base to the surrounding area. It is reported that he hated his job and wrote home to his family expressing this and that he had no idea what he was doing. He found solace, however, when he retired to his tent after a long day, where he would ponder philosophical matters.

He began experimenting and improved a process for cheaply making soda ash, a primary chemical used to manufacture glass, textiles, soap, and paper. His process was presented to some of France's leading scientists, but they declined to pursue it because they claimed it would not be cost-effective. Fresnel was crushed that his invention was rejected from being pursued, but that did not stop him from getting up and trying again on something else.

While on assignment on a major project in the South of France to build a road connecting Spain and Northern Italy, he turned his attention to the element that would change how he is remembered forever: light.[11]

---

[11] "A Short Bright Flash: Augustin Fresnel and the Birth of the Modern Lighthouse" by Theresa Levitt

Fresnel studied diffraction, which is the slight bending of light as it passes around the edge of an object.[12] "Diffraction" comes from the Latin word *diffringere,* meaning "to break into pieces."[13]

Fresnel found that when a beam of light passed through a small slit, it seemed to break apart and spread across the room, producing a pattern of light and dark much wider than either the original beam of light or the slit through which it had passed. This effect was made known in the seventeenth century, but it appears no one could fully explain how this phenomenon occurred.

Sir Isaac Newton had spent time investigating diffraction, concluding that light was made of particles that traveled in straight lines. His theory came to be known as the particle theory of light.

Fresnel, however, proposed that light was a wave rather than a particle, which aligned with the findings of Christian Huygens, who first came up with the wave theory of light in 1678.[14]

Fresnel began undertaking science experiments in 1814.[15] In his most precise experimental account of diffraction, he set up a dark room void of all light and completely blocked from the sun except for a very narrow beam coming through a hole he punched through a metal sheet on the outer wall. Fresnel used a large lens to focus the sun's light on the hole that was made to get the beam as bright as possible.

Inside the room, he then placed a metal wire in front of the light source, so it would cast its shadow on a white screen set on the wall opposite where the sun shone in. He rigged a triangular grid of silk thread, which he placed between his eyes and the wire, to measure the distances between

---

[12] http://ww2010.atmos.uiuc.edu/(Gh)/guides/mtr/opt/mch/diff.rxml

[13] https://www.vocabulary.com/dictionary/diffraction

[14] https://global.canon/en/technology/s_labo/light/001/11.html

[15] https://mathshistory.st-andrews.ac.uk/Biographies/Fresnel/

the shadow's fringes. After noting where the light and dark bands fell on the triangle, he used geometry to compute the width of the fringes. His observations matched his calculated predictions to .2 millimeters, leaving no doubt about the correctness of the formula he derived from the wave theory of light. He subsequently documented the results in a memoir he sent to his uncle in 1815. He would later use this powerful mathematical technique to propel him to greater heights in the scientific community.

THE GRAND PRIZE

In the spring of 1817, the French Academy of Sciences announced that the grand prize for its annual competition would be given for the best work on one of the most critical scientific problems of the day: *diffraction*.

Fresnel was one of the entrants. Although people who had entered the competition remained anonymous, it was easy to spot Fresnel's entry, as it was inscribed with the words *Natura simplex et fecunda* (nature simple and fertile), which presented the sole defense of his theory that light is a wave.

Fresnel had worked through twenty-five possible cases where diffraction patterns could be seen in an object's shadow, from thin wires to razors' edges. In each case, he calculated the expected intensity pattern of the shadows and then compared his predictions to his experimental results.

On April 20, 1818, Fresnel handed in his memoir and returned to his engineering work while he waited for the French Academy of Sciences to evaluate his memoir.

The committee of judges included several prominent advocates of the Newtonian view, one of whom was mathematician Simeon-Denis Poisson. He reasoned that if light was truly a wave, when a light was cast on a perfectly round object, the light waves would bend around the sides of the object. Using Fresnel's equations, he worked through an example that Fresnel had not yet tried, which predicted a seemingly laughable result: if a beam of light shines on a perfectly round object, there would be a bright, white spot in the middle of the circular shadow —a spot nearly as bright as if the obstacle was not there at all.

He and others appeared to revel in the idea that any theory yielding such an implausible result must certainly be wrong. They reasoned that if you took a light and shined it on a perfectly spherical object, the light rays, which they believed to be linear in nature, would create a circular shadow when they traveled just past the outside of the object. However, it would be impossible for a bright white spot to appear in the middle of the shadow.

The committee's initial negative response to Fresnel's entry merely spurred his ally, French physicist Francois Arago, to test Fresnel's theory!

The entire prize committee, including Simeon-Denis Poisson, assembled to watch a test of the diffraction pattern of a disc. They put together a light source, a disc, and a screen behind the object. When they shined the light on the disc, a shadow was cast on the screen that had been placed behind it. The committee of judges was not expecting to see anything in the middle of the shadow but what appeared in the center of the shadow was the very white spot in question. It was just as illuminated as if the screen did not exist. This proved Fresnel's seemingly impossible calculations had been right.

Fresnel was awarded the grand prize on March 15, 1819. At that moment, he was on the brink of revolutionizing the science of light.[16]

---

[16] "A Short Bright Flash: Augustin Fresnel and the Birth of the Modern Lighthouse" by Theresa Levitt

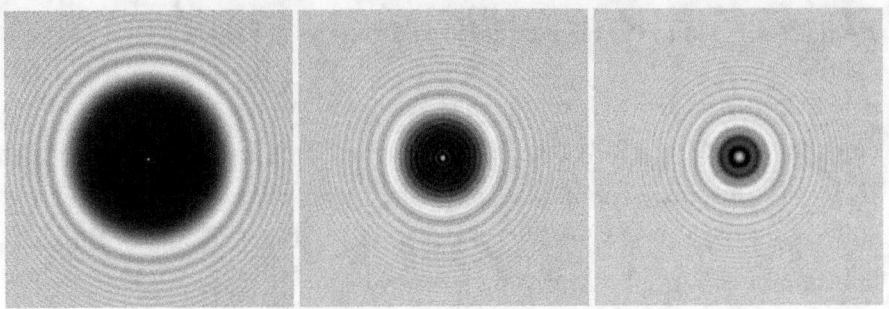

Arago spots in the shadow of a disc of varying diameter
(4 mm, 2 mm, 1 mm – left to right) at a distance of 1 m from the disc.[17]

Shortly after, he was appointed to a team to assist in lighthouse design—to improve the quality and quantity of the light emitted to save lives along the coastlines.

I love how Fresnel pushed through even when the days were dark. He was dealing with his own physical ailments. Yet, he still chose to move forward in the face of rejection when members of the French Academy of Sciences had concluded that his theory of light being a wave was implausible. Fresnel had even been considered an imposter, as some assumed he was stealing physicist Thomas Young's theory. But when asked about Thomas Young, Fresnel replied, "Who?"

Despite the difficulties he faced, he had the support of those who believed in him and knew he had something special to offer. He never gave up, even when he probably felt like he was going to break.

**Usually, a person feels like they are going to break
right before they experience their breakthrough.**

And Fresnel certainly did.

---

[17] https://en.wikipedia.org/wiki/Arago_spot

EARLY LIGHTHOUSES AND ILLUMINATION

The first known lighthouse was the Pharos of Alexandria, Egypt.[18] It was constructed between 300 and 280 B.C. by Ptolemy I and his son Ptolemy II. It was illuminated by flames provided by an open wood fire and was also one of the Seven Wonders of the Ancient World. Many of the early lighthouses produced light from an open wood fire, later followed by fire beacons secured in an iron basket or grate called a brazier. Coal fires were used to illuminate lighthouses beginning in the 17th century, followed by candles in the 18th century, and finally oil lamps in the 19th century— during Fresnel's time.

With each era that passed, the goal had always been illumination. With the number of tragic deaths caused by shipwrecks near the shore, the focus changed to not just illumination but a projection of the illumination into the night. Before Fresnel's invention, mirrors had been placed behind lamps to reflect as much light outward as possible. These were called reflectors.

The problem was that even the most flawless mirror lost half its light on reflection, causing too much light to escape.

Because of its low integrity or inability to remain whole and undivided, the light emitted from a lighthouse only could travel a few miles out to sea. This meant that by the time a ship could see the light, they were already courting calamity.

FRESNEL'S SOLUTION

Fresnel noticed this problem and decided to solve it by replacing reflectors with lenses. Initially, the idea of using a lens instead of reflectors seemed grand, but there also appeared to be a fatal flaw in implementing them.

---

[18] https://www.pointarenalighthouse.com/about/general-lighthouse-facts-and-the-history-of-illumination/

The lens needed to be placed very close to the light source to capture as much light as possible. This meant that "the rays of light would have to be refracted through a very large angle to get them parallel with one another, in order to create a bright light." [19]

A giant lens with a middle much thicker than its edges was required. The flaw was in the thickness of the proposed lens. The thicker the middle, the greater the amount of light that was lost passing through it. The thicker the lens, the heavier it was as well, and a giant lens with a thick middle would be too heavy for any kind of machinery to hold and rotate.

But then a genius idea struck Fresnel.

Theresa Levitt writes in her book, *A Short Bright Flash: Augustin Fresnel and the Birth of the Modern Lighthouse:*

"Fresnel then thought of a way to create a giant lens without all of the bulk in the middle: construct it in steps. Break the single curved surface into several concentric sections consisting of distinct prisms or triangular pieces of glass that would refract the light. Each of these individual prisms would bend the light rays from their source into a parallel line."

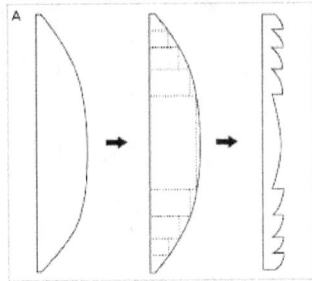

In other words, using refraction, also known as the bending of light, a Fresnel Lens, which consisted of several concentric sections of cut glass or

---

[19] "A Short Bright Flash: Augustin Fresnel and the Birth of the Modern Lighthouse" by Theresa Levitt

prisms, could take all the light emanating from the source and channel it in the same direction. This permitted the light to intensify and bend in such a way that it would penetrate the night over 20 miles out to sea.

Now, mariners would have time to change course before getting too close to the shore!

Fresnel saved countless lives because of his work.

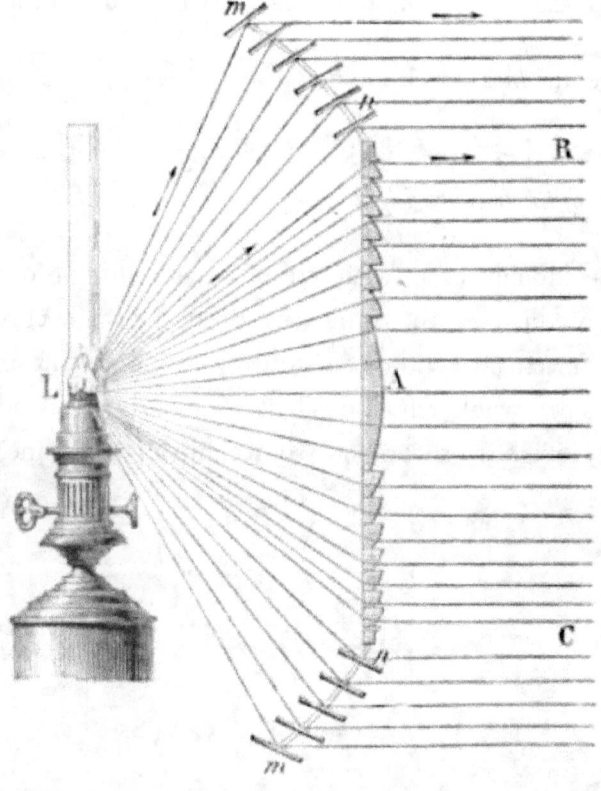

20

He went on to design six sizes of lenses, which were divided into four orders depending on their focal length and size. In modern use, these orders are classified as the first through sixth order.[21] The largest Fresnel Lenses are known as "hyperradiant." One of these lenses was even used to outfit the Mapapuu Point Lighthouse in Ohahu, Hawaii. When my twin sister and her husband visited there last year, they sent me a picture of that very lighthouse.

I immediately spotted the Fresnel Lens and gasped—the lighthouse, kissed by the sun, rested on what looked like a shady mountain or volcano. Almost half the body of the lighthouse was wrapped in glass windows so the lens could be seen. The lower half of the shell appeared to be white stucco. After reading about this particular lighthouse, I learned the design used over a thousand prisms!

The prisms inside the lighthouse cause the light to pierce the night. It is the reason the light can shine so brightly and reach so far into the dark.

As the prism is an integral part of the lighthouse, it will also be one of the critical elements we will discuss later in this book.

While I am not an expert on the Fresnel Lens, I have so enjoyed learning about this magnificent invention. I know now that we can draw parallels between lighthouses and our own light.

First, and of utmost importance, is:

The light within you is greater than the darkness outside you. Remember that when you can't see farther than your fingertips.

---

[21] https://en.wikipedia.org/wiki/Fresnel_lens

Keep your focus on the light inside you, for the light within you is always there. The light within you comes from your inheritance because you are made in the image of God!

1 John 1:5 says, "…God is light; in Him there is no darkness at all." You are a child of light. Even if you feel like your light is only flickering, it's still on.

Second, there is power in how you direct your light.

Just as the Fresnel Lens bends the light on the inside to direct it straight out, there's power in how you direct your light. We will get more into this when we go through Step 4 of the Lighthouse Method, *How to Bend Your Light and Shine.*

Finally, live with integrity, so your light does not escape.

By definition, integrity is "the state of being whole and not divided."[22] Living with integrity is vital to preventing your light from escaping. When you live without integrity, you can think you're shining, but you're not. When we allow our light to escape, we lose the quality of our light. It becomes diluted, and we can't shine as brightly.

Lighthouses have evolved over the years. In this book, when I reference lighthouse lenses, I am speaking of what Fresnel created. I am not speaking about other attributes or traits of lighthouses before or after the Fresnel Lens. Fresnel created a pivotal moment in history for lighthouses, and his invention saved millions of lives. The same can be said for someone choosing to light up the world, particularly after a traumatic incident.

And think about this: *What if that person is you?*

---

[22] https://www.oxfordlearnersdictionaries.com/us/definition/american_english/integrity

CHAPTER 3

The Lighthouse Purpose and Method

"The people living in the darkness have seen a great light; on those living in the land of the shadow of death a light has dawned."

—Matthew 4:16

You were made to rise. You were made to stand firm against outside forces.

You were made to offer Harbor for the lost.

Just like a lighthouse.

Before diving into The Lighthouse Method steps, I want to highlight specific lighthouse attributes and traits. These will help you visualize the purpose of a lighthouse so it can help you see yours. There are many differences between you and a lighthouse, and there are also many similarities. Let's explore them together.

LIGHTHOUSE ATTRIBUTES

As I shared with you earlier, I have related to lighthouses because of their various attributes, dating as far back as I can remember. I have also seen myself in them. For starters, a lighthouse:

Allows you to see your location from their lights.

When you are standing in the dark, you cannot see where you are. When you can't see where you are, it is impossible to see where you should go. When you are standing in the dark, you could take steps, thinking you are moving forward, only to realize you are moving in a circle. Without light, you don't know where "forward" actually is.

Allows you to see its location from their lights.

With light, you can see how close you are to Harbor. This enables hope to rise up, giving you the courage to keep going.

You can identify hazards.

It is impossible to see clearly in the dark. Without light, you cannot see the rocks ahead that can harm you. With light, you can see. With light, you may also have an awareness of a crippling behavior or relationship.

All the pieces of the lighthouse must work in conjunction to shine.

Just as a Fresnel Lens in a lighthouse cannot work properly without the assistance of other supportive material, including things like prisms, mercury, or a hand-wound clock (which has since been replaced with an electric motor) to aid with lens rotation, you cannot shine without the support of others.

LIGHTHOUSE TRAITS

They are circular and can withstand force from all directions.

It's important for our bodies to be whole and strong enough to withstand forces, too—no matter where they come from.

Lighthouses are generally very tall structures, allowing the light to be seen further out.

Be tall and complete—set yourself in a high place. We are set in a high place as citizens of Heaven living on Earth. This is who we are designed to be.

Lighthouses are positioned near the shoreline.

Lighthouses were designed to be built on shorelines to warn mariners of dangerous shallows and perilous rocky coasts. You were also placed in a position to offer light to a mariner who may be sailing too close to a perilous rocky coast, but if you are not positioned correctly—mind, body, spirit—if you are not healed, you cannot offer Harbor to that mariner.

I shared the lighthouse attributes and traits with you because it leads to the explanation of The Lighthouse Method, a method that I believe will help you shine again as it did me. With the whole picture, you can appreciate the many parallels between yourself and a lighthouse before diving into the steps of The Lighthouse Method.

STEPS TO THE LIGHTHOUSE METHOD

STEP 1: PREPARE TO RISE UP

"To be prepared is half the victory."

—Miguel De Cervantes

A lighthouse is a massive tower rising high above the land. It can withstand outside forces because it is whole, inside and out. Just like a lighthouse, you must rise above your circumstances and choices. You must rise out of the valley of the shadow of death. And you must be complete to do what you were designed to do—shine!

Like anything you do in life, you cannot reach your goal of rising without preparation. Preparation is defined as "the action or process of making ready or being made ready for use or consideration." It is also defined as "Something done to get ready for an event or undertaking.[23]"

Preparation is a process—and one that begins in the mind.

CAST THE VISION

Any person who desires to live in victory must first see themselves living victoriously.

Think of some of the greats throughout history—well before Leonardo da Vinci painted *The Last Supper*, he saw the masterpiece in his mind. Before sisters Serena and Venus Williams became tennis legends, they saw themselves as champions. They cast the vision.

The same can be said of a person looking to rise from the darkness of depression. Any person who desires to rise must first see themselves risen. If you see it, you can become it.

Dr. Moses Simuyemba states, "Your vision is limited only by you. See yourself as the truly capable human being that you are."

If you cannot see yourself as the truly capable human that you are—if you cannot see yourself risen—you will always remain on the ground, an incomplete mess. No one really wants to stay that way.

You don't have to feel it—just see it so you can begin going there. The very act of seeing yourself in a higher place takes you higher, even if you can't tap into that emotion.

---

[23] https://www.lexico.com/en/definition/preparation

COMMIT TO TAKING REGULAR ACTIONS TO STAY HEALTHY

After you cast your vision internally, commit to taking regular actions to stay healthy. I cannot stress enough how important this is!

"You cannot conquer what you are not committed to."

—T.D. Jakes

When you fill your time with what is good for your mind, body, and spirit, you naturally won't have time for what is not good for you—like marinating in a bottle of vodka (or a tub of ice cream) and self-condemning thoughts. These are ingredients to a recipe for disaster. Vices are simply unhealthy and will prolong your healing.

Instead, set yourself up for victory by taking action on what will help you get to where you desire to be, including, in no particular order:

Exercise

Get your body moving, or you'll be months down the road, still wallowing in depression with no progress. Yes, you can move in the dark! At least you're moving! When you exercise, chemicals are released in the body that can help improve your mood, enhance your sense of well-being, and assist in relaxation. Exercise has also been shown to help with stress and reduce a person's risk of depression.[24]

Prayer

This may be the last thing you want to do because you may not feel like you deserve peace. But prayer brings peace! It brings an inward stillness and is a place where you acknowledge that you are not alone. In prayer, you can cry out for help! Angels are put on assignment with your request.

---

[24] https://medlineplus.gov/benefitsofexercise.html

Vice.com recounts the results of a study done between 2005 and 2008, in which retired pediatrician Peter Boelens prayed with 27 men and women for one hour per week for six weeks. Every person in this group study was clinically depressed. At the end of six weeks, each person's scores on the Hamilton Rating Scales for Depression and Anxiety had decreased.[25]

Fill Your Cup

It is imperative that you fill your mind with light if you want to project it. This means filling your cup with the right ingredients, like reading your Bible and listening to a podcast on overcoming.

1. Read the Bible

This is one of the ways God will speak to you. As you read intentionally, you will notice the words jumping off the page, connecting with your heart. You may find yourself crying or filled with boldness after reading. That is the work of the Holy Spirit, who is your Comforter.

2. Listen to a Podcast on Overcoming

You are not alone. You are not the only person in existence to feel the way you do. You are not the only person who has messed up. We all have. Stop listening to that inner voice that continues to criticize you. Instead, listen to another's story. Just like you are doing here by reading this book, find a podcast that speaks to you—on overcoming or leadership or anything positive. Make sure it fills you with inspiration. Scott Barry Kaufman notes that inspiration will "awaken us to new possibilities by allowing us to transcend our ordinary experiences and limitations. Inspiration propels a person from apathy to possibility, and transforms the way we perceive our own capabilities."

---

[25] https://www.vice.com/en/article/nzpk9w/how-prayer-and-meditation-changes-your-brain

May committing to taking these actions to stay healthy propel you forward with a renewed sense of hope.

HONOR YOUR EMOTIONS

Honoring your emotions means you must feel pain, grief, anger, and heartache and process them to heal. Don't let these feelings control you. This is the difference between the waves of depression pulling you under or the waves merely lapping at you as you swim to shore.

Molly Friedenfeld says, "We can honor our emotions after any traumatic event by moving through the experience centered in the heart with the goal of reaching the light on the other side."

When you don't allow your emotions to dictate your self-worth, stop condemning yourself repeatedly, and choose to feel rather than suppress what you are feeling by attempting to turn off your emotions, you are on the fast track to healing.

FIGHT TO RECLAIM YOUR LIFE

Fighting involves making the choice to do hard things! This means facing your fear, rejection, and the people you hurt or the people who hurt you.

As you go about finding yourself again, remember that you *can* recover what was lost!

Your life is not over. You must choose to fight!

Swim.

Rise up!

Say to the darkness, "You have no hold on me!" The choices you made do not define you or dictate your future. You are not what has been spoken over you by others. You are not the words you have spoken over yourself.

You can choose to rise out of this seemingly bottomless pit—and find a world of color waiting for you on the other side of your brokenness.

You *will* breathe again.

Fix your eyes on the surface, find the resolve, and swim. Your future depends on it.

> *"When the going gets tough, put one foot in front of the other and just keep going. Don't give up."*
>
> —Roy T. Bennett

BORROW ANOTHER'S LIGHT

If you absolutely do not think you can find your light, borrow another's just until you are healed enough to shine again. It's okay—borrowing another's light can be a lifeline when you don't think you have the headspace to take those first steps to get out of your darkness. The beauty of doing this is that it forces you to get close enough to someone else's light instead of sitting in isolation. Solitude is necessary in certain instances, but you cannot stay there forever. This should be your last resort.

Ella Baker said, "Give light, and people will find the way." If others give you their light, you can find your way. A word of caution, though...

If you borrow another's light to jumpstart your healing journey, set a time limit on how long you will hold onto it. You won't produce your light by osmosis or through holding your neighbor's. When you return their light, you'll be back in the dark unless you have taken the first steps out of it.

You may have noticed that much of this first step is internal. This step is where the battle is because it is in your mind. Right now, you must decide who wins.

If you can commit to this first step, you can complete the rest of them.

STEP 2: BECOME A PRISM

"When you possess light within you, you see it externally."

— Anas Nin

When a ray of light passes through a prism, the color that emerges from it is nothing short of miraculous. It is a spectrum of vividness suddenly appearing out of nowhere. Sometimes you may see a prism appear in the corner of your living room or kitchen, dancing on the floor or walls, bringing a reminder of hope.

That's what rainbows do.

When light passes through a lighthouse prism, what emerges is also miraculous—except, in this case, it is not a spectrum of color but a vibrant band of light.

This is why the prism is one of the most important components of the lighthouse, particularly the ones that were used during Fresnel's time.

The Fresnel Lens is made of many transparent prisms which allow light emanating from it to become visible. When an object is transparent, you can see through it. With this quality, a prism allows light to pass through it and shine out into the night.

Close your eyes for a moment and picture a prism in your mind. What do you see? I see a triangular-shaped piece of glass. I see several of them actually dangling in front of the face of actress Hayley Mills in the prism scene of the 1960 movie *Pollyanna*. If you're not sure what scene this is, just Google "prism scene Pollyana" and a video will pop right up. In this scene, the prisms were not only beautiful pieces of glass. Because of their transparency, light could pass through the prisms and cast tiny rainbows on a wall on the other side of the room.

Lighthouses may not cast rainbows, but they can cast a vibrant band of light out into the night— because of the prism.

A prism as we know it doesn't always start in the way we imagine, though. Before it becomes a beautiful creation, the material that makes up a prism must go through a purification process. Let me explain.

GLASS

A prism is typically made of glass. Most glass is made by combining sand, soda ash, and limestone and melting these elements at a very high temperature. These raw materials, as you might suspect, contain impurities that cannot be present to create the brilliance needed for a lighthouse lens.[26]

When these impurities are heated, they melt away, and the body of dirt and debris transforms into a beautiful, pristine, and sustaining creation.

During Fresnel's time, the earliest prisms were made of lead crystal glass, but they were found to chip easily. If you ever have the chance to see an old Fresnel Lens, look closely, and you will see chips on the edges of many of them. It's interesting to note that after a period of time trying to resolve the chipping problem, sodium was added to the glass when it was made. The new product was called "crown glass." If you ever see it in person, you'll note it has a slightly greenish hue but is much less likely to chip.[27]

TRANSPARENT

Prisms are transparent, allowing light waves to pass through so objects behind them can be clearly seen. When we allow ourselves to be purified, light passes through us and out into the night. The purification steps are explained in greater depth a little later in this book, but I will list them below:

---

[26] https://www.glassallianceeurope.eu/en/what-is-glass
[27] http://pajack.com/lighthouses/more-lighthouse-info/the-amazing-fresnel-lens/

PURIFICATION STEPS

1. Humility

Recognize that you are still learning and that being a person trying to live up to how God sees you is hard. Commit to learning and not chastising yourself for not knowing every right decision. If you have been wronged, be so humble that you can learn to see how better to protect yourself.

2. Confession

Speak out about what you did and make no excuses. There's no need to punish yourself and berate yourself or others exhaustively. Accept the situation for its truth and release. You will feel a huge sense of relief in owning your behavior and words.

3. Repentance

To repent means, you will feel regret; this is normal and healthy. What is not is to stay in this place of recrimination. Take seriously what you did to the degree that you will do everything in your power never to do it again. Further, you will use these new skills to make optimal decisions for you and everyone around you going forward.

4. Forgiveness

When you live in a state of unforgiveness, whether you need to forgive yourself or others, you contain your light. You continue to punish yourself—even if you are not the catalyst for putting yourself in this dark place. But you will stay in this acrimony and emotional agony until you release the hold of unforgiveness.

5. Replacement

Learning to love and move on positively requires a new focus, a rewiring of the habits of your mind and the voices you allow in your head. What will you use to replace your feelings of shame? How will you train yourself to think about what you have done or what's been done to you? Do you need to change who's in your life or your environment? Replacement means the changing out of the old in favor of the new.

As you are postured (the attitude in your heart[28]) in humility, if you confess your sins or wrongdoings, repent of them, forgive yourself and/or others, and then replace the lies about who you think you are with the truth of who God says you are, the result is a mindset shift.

Transparency changes how we view ourselves and the world. It gives us the ability to create a vibration that ripples from the inside to the outside of ourselves and into the world around us.

HARNESS LIGHT

Prisms harness and intensify light by gathering and directing it at a target. Harnessing light complements transparency because when you allow others to see through you, you become a conduit for light. This light then intensifies as it passes through you and out into the world around you.

Similarly, as light passes through a Fresnel Lens, the light bends, and the light rays intensify and unify in the same direction, permitting the light to reach deep into the night.

When light passes through you, you can change the world. This is why this step in the Lighthouse Method is the most essential. A person must become a prism for their light to have the ability to pierce the night.

---

[28] physio-pedia.com/posture

STEP 3: HAVE THE RIGHT SUPPORT SYSTEM
•••

"Be strong, be fearless, be beautiful. And believe that anything is possible when you have the right people there to support you."

—Misty Copeland

When we think of a lighthouse, our focus tends to be on the light coming from it, or maybe it is on the tower of stone resting so beautifully over a landscape. We likely call up these images because we can physically see them. But we often forget about the value in the hidden traits or qualities. We must remember the parts inside the lighthouse that are working and supporting it. Without these components, there would be no light.

The Fresnel Lens used elements to support it, including:

Mercury Bath – The mercury bath was first installed at Cape La Heve, France, in 1893.[29] It consisted of a donut-shaped basin containing a small amount of mercury, a heavy silvery-white metal that becomes liquid at ordinary temperatures.[30] Attached to the base of a lens was a large ring supported by, and also submerged in, the mercury, which was placed in the basin. This assembly allowed the speed of rotation of the Fresnel Lens to be increased dramatically and the ability to operate in a nearly friction-less environment. As a result, lenses weighing several tons could be started in motion with the push of a single finger.[31]

Prisms – Some Fresnel Lenses can be regarded as an array of prisms arranged circularly, with steeper prisms on the edges and a flat or slightly convex middle. In earlier versions of the lens, each section was a separate prism. Later versions included "single-piece" lenses. However, it took time

---

[29] https://uslhs.org/lens-rotation

[30] https://www.google.com/search?q=mercury+definition

[31] https://uslhs.org/lens-rotation#:~:text=The%20mercury%20bath%20allowed %20the,rotation%20to%20be%20dramatically%20increased.

for the later version to take hold because the glass seemed to break or bubble too much during formation.[32]

Metal Stand – This held the prisms in place.

Clockwork Mechanics – These allowed the light source to rotate and sweep across a much greater area of the sea. Rotation made the light appear to flash every so often. In Fresnel's day, lighthouses flashed at different rates, which made it easier for sailors to figure out which lighthouse they were looking at when they timed the flashes. This also helped them pinpoint exactly where they were.

Bull's Eye Panel – A Fresnel Lens started as a larger piece of glass cut down to its useful, refracting outer edge. The lens wrapped itself around a light source and had concentric rings that looked like steps or thick ridges on its surface. Visually, it looked similar to a bull's eye. Each step bent the light a little more than the one beneath it, enabling all the light rays to emerge in a bright, powerful beam that could shine many miles out to sea.

These support elements, and many others, working together allowed the light to shine from a Fresnel Lens.

SUPPORT IN YOUR LIFE

Your light will not shine in your life unless you have the right support holding you up. When you realize others are there to help you succeed, a natural surrendering takes place, and you will welcome the support.

The difference between a lighthouse and its support is that the lighthouse has no choice whether the support is there. The makers of lighthouses made sure the supportive elements were in place because they were needed for the lighthouse to give off light.

---

[32] https://www.missionpointlighthouse.com/the-fresnel-lens.html

You, however, have a choice. You can choose who surrounds you. You can choose if no one surrounds you. And if you choose the latter path, well, it will be impossible for your light to shine the way it was designed to.

My advice to you is to make that brave choice to have people around you and accept help from Heaven.

Tess Guinery speaks so beautifully on the opportunity to make a brave choice in her book, *The Apricot Memoirs:*

> "Sometimes we get given the opportunity to make a brave choice. To surrender the things that are great for the things that are greater. It's here a soulful, lively, boom-boom, heart out of chest, tears on cheeks, I'm alive kind of passion lives—it lives, just around the corner from surrender's bend."

Accepting help is not a weakness. Instead, it shows great strength when someone surrenders their will for something greater.

Will you, then, surrender?

Will you surrender what you think is best for you?

Will you surrender the "I will go it alone" mindset?

Will you just surrender?

During war, one of the universal signs of surrendering is putting your hands in the air. This indicates that you hold no weapons and have nothing to hide.

You will also see people doing this in many churches during worship as an act of reverence for God, and people have different reasons for doing it. Sometimes they are putting their hands up in surrender—surrendering their way, laying all their burdens at the feet of the cross. They have realized they have been seeking happiness in all the wrong places. Other times, they may be putting their hands up to receive the love of God. Either way, they are acknowledging that they need God. They are accepting the help that Heaven may bring.

THE RIGHT SUPPORT

We've now determined the importance of support in your life. Now, let's focus on the *right* kind of support for you.

When I look back on key moments in my life that either positively or negatively impacted me, it all came down to the people in my life who were surrounding me.

This always makes me think of a line Pastor Jacob Aranza says when he is preaching on relationships:

> **"Tell me who your five closest friends are,
> and I'll tell you who you are."**

Aranza means that the people you surround yourself with will influence you, whether you admit it or not.

This can be a very good thing or a very bad thing.

If your five closest friends lack initiative, have difficulty keeping a good job, and speak badly of their spouses, I hate to break it to you, but you will likely find yourself living very similar to them. On the flip side, what if your five closest friends are ambitious entrepreneurs, highly successful in business, and treat their spouses with respect? Then you will most likely find yourself being and doing these kinds of things, too.

1 Corinthians 15:33 tells us, "Bad company corrupts good morals," and Proverbs 18:24 says, "One who has unreliable friends soon comes to ruin, but there is a friend who sticks closer than a brother."

Who, then, is the right support for you? Simply, the right supportive people for you will:

- Believe in you.

- Teach you.

- Challenge you.

- Validate you.

- Love you.

You want these kinds of people in your corner. Think about the people in your life right now. Can you name five people who want to support you?

- Do they believe in you?

- Do they teach you?

- Do they challenge you?

- Do they validate you?

- Do they love you?

If these people do not carry most, if not all, these traits, they're not the right support; it's time to find someone else to replace them. Replacing support may cause you to lose some relationships, and that may hurt for a time. But when you say "No" to something, you're also saying "Yes" to something else. Make sure you have the right people in your life. Otherwise, you can cast the vision for being risen all day long, but you will not have the capacity to shine. Just like a lighthouse cannot shine without the supportive elements assisting the Fresnel Lens, you cannot shine unless you have the right support around you.

STEP 4: LEARN HOW TO BEND YOUR LIGHT AND SHINE
••

"Where there is darkness, let there be light."

—Francis of Assisi

In the previous steps, you have been making a way for your light to be emitted. In this step, your light will intensify and shine out across the dense fog of your life. As light passes through a Fresnel Lens, the light bends, and the light rays unify in the same direction.

This bending of light is known as refraction. It occurs when light passes from one transparent medium to another. In the case of a Fresnel Lens, refraction happens when light passes from air to glass.

This is *how* it occurs. But what about what happens *when* it occurs? That's the most amazing part of all.

When light passes through a Fresnel Lens, the path of a light ray changes direction. After you become a prism and light can pass through you, your light will change direction! You will change direction.

Is this mere thought blowing your mind yet as it did mine?

Now, let's get nerdier!

The meeting place where light encounters a medium different than the one through which it has been traveling is the interface. All refraction of light occurs at the interface!

In layman's terms, the interface is where the change happens. This is when transformation occurs. You can also detect a visible change from the outside. You are the same. When you go through a transformation, others notice it.

In a lighthouse, the interface is the place where light touches the prisms. Once the light passes from air to glass, due to its transparent qualities, the light can pass through and change direction at the same time.

What, then, is the interface for a person causing them to change direction? It is the lens through which they see—the lens through which they can be seen. The transformation will not occur unless you are transparent or light can pass through you. Refraction cannot take place.

Transparency is the condition of being see-through and is an inside job.

In a lighthouse, the transparent prisms are on the inside. Transparency happens on the inside.

The bending of light and change in the direction of light happens at the transparent interface.

Your interface must also be transparent for your light to pierce the night.

Again, your interface is the lens through which you see—the lens through which others can see you. This is why it is important that your lens is transparent and not clouded or muddied by your choices or circumstances.

Just as prisms harness and intensify light by gathering light and directing it at a target—when you allow yourself to be see-through, you are a conduit for light. Your light intensifies as it passes through you and into the world.

STEP 5: FIND HARBOR AND BECOME IT

"For I believe in harbors at the end."

—Thomas Wolfe

When you have gone through the Lighthouse Method Steps 1–4, you can seek Harbor because the light has reached you. At this moment, you will rise out of the waters of depression, anxiety, and fear that have sought to take your life. This is when you will courageously begin your steps to the shore.

This may sound slightly counterintuitive since we just spent the first few chapters discussing how to shine again after losing your light.

I have painted the picture for you of becoming a prism so your light can shine out into the night. The purpose of shining is so light can reach the lost mariner.

Well, that lost mariner is you.

And now you are found.

Have you seen the movie, *Safe Haven*? It is a 2013 film centered around a young woman's move to a small town on the North Carolina coast, where she makes a new life for herself. She had come from an abusive relationship and had no longer felt safe where she was. When she moved to the small town on the coast, she was soon won over by the warmth of the close-knit community and found safety in that place.

It was there she found Harbor.

Harbor is defined as "A place on the coast where vessels may find shelter, especially one protected from rough water by piers, jetties, and other artificial structures."[33]

In this definition, we can see that Harbor is a place.

---

[33] https://www.lexico.com/en/definition/harbor

Psalm 107:23-32 speaks of God leading us to Harbor:

> Some of you set sail in big ships;
>
>> you put to sea to do business in faraway ports.
>
> Out at sea you saw God in action,
>
>> saw his breathtaking ways with the ocean:
>
> With a word he called up the wind—
>
>> an ocean storm, towering waves!
>
> You shot high in the sky, then the bottom dropped out;
>
>> your hearts were stuck in your throats.
>
> You were spun like a top, you reeled like a drunk,
>
>> you didn't know which end was up.
>
> Then you called out to God in your desperate condition;
>
>> he got you out in the nick of time.
>
> He quieted the wind down to a whisper,
>
>> put a muzzle on all the big waves.
>
> And you were so glad when the storm died down,
>
>> and he led you safely back to Harbor.
>
> So thank God for his marvelous love,
>
>> for his miracle mercy to the children he loves.
>
> Lift high your praises when the people assemble,
>
>> shout Hallelujah when the elders meet!"

I love this passage! When we cry out to God, he quiets our storms. He leads us safely back to Harbor.

This is a place any lost person being tossed about by their rocky circumstances desires to be.

**Another definition of Harbor shows it as being a "shelter."
It can be used as a verb ("to shelter") or as a noun ("a shelter").
Harbor is not only where you can find shelter,
but you can *be* the shelter.**

Reaching Harbor gets you to a safe place where you learn that your light was never meant to be just for you. Your light is for the world. Your fight was not just for you to win, either. Your win empowers generations to win. It has a rippling effect.

Your breakthrough happens during Step 5 of The Lighthouse Method. All the steps you have been through have built on each other to bring you to this moment. Now you can look at the darkness without fear creeping in because you have learned to take authority over it.

Because you are moving.

You can feel yourself getting lighter and ascending. Your world isn't one of hoping or preparing for the hope that you will come out of the gray. Instead, you will see yourself moving toward the light.

This is what victory looks like!

WALKING TO SHORE

During the Harbor Phase:

- You come back from your setback.
- You stand tall in your identity.
- You tell your story.
- You rescue another mariner lost at sea.

Once you are found.

Once you have healed.

Once you rise up, you become who you were destined to be—a Harbor for the lost.

Because you have reached Harbor, you can now offer Harbor to someone else.

You do this by standing on the shoreline of your life, with feet planted firmly on the ground. You look out over the waters around you for another person who needs to be rescued. You will become the person they most desperately need to find. You may be the one who saves them from going under the waves of depression that are trying to pull them under. You may be the one who introduces them to the One who can save their soul.

If not you, then who?

CHAPTER 4

LOST AT SEA

*"And when she dreams, she dreams of a girl who
was lost at sea but one day found the shore."*

—Gabrielle Zevin

I found myself living in the "in between." In between life. In between death. In the gray. I floated in a colorless realm, lulled to sleep by the rocking of the waves.

Lost at sea.

I was living there because I had drifted off course.

I was living there because I actually believed I deserved to be there, unable to move under the grappling weight of my choices.

I remember floating in the water. I remember feeling numb. I remember the darkness.

WHEN I WAS LOST

During my first year of law school, there were many days when I felt like I did not belong. I was an English major, a literature lover, and creative—

the world of law seemed like an unnatural path for me to take. I wasn't the typical pre-law major. Before setting foot on campus, I had never heard words like "personal jurisdiction" or any kind of "diction," for that matter. All I knew was that the job I found myself in post-college was not where I was destined to be; I was cleaning toilets at a gym.

I vividly remember the day I became determined to do more with my education. I woke up knowing there was so much untapped potential resting in my mind and life—that if I didn't do more with what was in me, I would always feel restless. That I hadn't done enough.

I chose law partly because of the potential financial security I thought being an attorney could offer me. I also enjoyed the way the written word was analyzed and dissected in law school, which was a strength for me.

I took the Law School Admission Test (LSAT) on my birthday. The LSAT is a standardized test administered several times each year at designated testing centers throughout the world. A person takes this test to determine if they can make it into law school. I'd love to relay that I set a record and passed with flying colors, which is how I was used to performing. The truth is I simply got by with an average score—but it was enough.

Before classes started, I went to the law school's library and checked out audio tapes on Civil Procedure and other classes. It's not that I wanted to outrank everyone. While it's in my nature to do well, I just did not want to appear as a yellow-striped minnow among the other adult fish.

In law school, they call the first-year students "1Ls," the second-year students "2Ls," and the third-year students "3Ls." When you are a 1L, everyone hates you. At least that's what it felt like. I learned later that the professors are so hard on the first-year students because they want to weed out the weak.

DAY ONE

On my first day, in my very first class, I was called on to speak. Now, law school is not like college. You can't just sit in your chair and take notes. You have to participate—and you never know when the professor may call on you.

The first time I was called on was that day.

Of course.

Mr. Smith was the first student to be interrogated with several questions regarding the material we were instructed to read before the first day of class. The professor then proceeded to drill the next several students sitting to Mr. Smith's right side.

Guess who was sitting right next to Mr. Smith? Me. Guilty by association.

The next few minutes under the professor's interrogation were a blur. I recall answering questions—some right, most wrong. But at least I knew that after the professor was done with me, my turn would not come back around in that class for over 100 days (since there were over 100 students in our class).

I had survived.

As time progressed that year, I found myself not only surviving but thriving. I did not feel like a weed ready to be pulled but a flower planted deeply in the soil. In the spring of my first year, I won the Best Paper Award in my section of my Legal Writing class.

I finally felt like I could be "one of them"—as if I weren't an outsider to the other students any longer. I wish I could have bottled up that feeling because only a few months later, the floor fell out from under my feet.

It was as if I was suspended in air, watching someone else's life unfold. This couldn't have been mine.

But it was.

My writing gift—handed to me by God—that had brought me much joy in one season brought immense grief in another.

MY WRITING GIFT

As a child, I loved resting in the realm of the imagination, getting lost in a book, and finding myself in its pages. In the thick of the makings of my own world, my heart connected so deeply to the written word. I knew early on that my gift would live in this realm of imagination, as I naturally gravitated toward it.

It was out of this connection that I began to write. Anywhere and everywhere, I felt inspired, whether it was under the dimly lit lamplight in my bedroom, on vacation while sitting out on the pier at our family camp, or even in between tests at school.

Writing was a form of breathing. It allowed me to inhale and exhale in a slow, steady way. It always took me to a place where I could search the deepest parts of myself, lather the tip of my pen with the most heartfelt human emotion and then transfer it to the reader through the words on the page.

Sometimes the reader was only me.

Writing was undoubtedly the most natural undertaking I had ever done in my life. Everything else, it seemed, took lots and lots of work.

For example, it took a long time for me to understand the mechanics of how one's body should move when running. Until I was an adult, I somehow never grasped the concept that I was supposed to bend my knees.

My father always said I was the fastest person he ever met… who ran without bending their legs! Let me take this moment to profusely apologize to every coach I ever had in athletics. I was really trying!

I also had a lisp as a child, which made it difficult to say my *S's* correctly for a long time. A lisp is considered a speech defect in which *s* is pronounced like the "th" in "thick." I recall a specialist coming to take me out of class at school when I was in the first grade to teach me to speak properly. Even with that aid, as I got older, I was embarrassed by the sounds coming out of my mouth—sounds that could roll so easily off others' tongues. If you had asked me back then to say, "Sally sold seashells by the seashore," I would have turned red in the face.

As I ponder this particular time in my life, I would surmise that one of the reasons I gravitated to the written word so much outside of my natural gift is that I would have rather read and write than speak.

Lisps didn't exist in books and in my imagination.

I was the valedictorian of my 8th-grade class. For my speech, I wrote a poem to conclude my presentation. The poem was something about the class setting sail on a ship and embarking on the future. It was heartfelt and lovely. I remember looking out in the crowd and seeing mothers crying. They were visibly moved by the words I was speaking. I noticed then the power in words, and I carried this love for the written word into high school and college, winning writing awards alongside other academic and athletic awards.

FALLING

During my second year in law school, I chose to take a writing class—one I was very excited about. We were given our topic over the Christmas break: Fraud.

I've got this, I thought confidently. I figured I was finally taking another class I could do well in. Not just average but well.

We were supposed to have our drafts ready when we returned from Christmas break. I had done the research and typed fourteen pages of notes. Without properly citing other authors' words in that draft, I submitted it, thinking *I'll have a proper paper ready by the time I need to submit the final.*

I know what I did was wrong. I took credit for someone else's words instead of creating my own.

In other words, I plagiarized.

"Plagiarism"—it's an ugly word.

As a person who had written countless papers before then—I was a literature major—I most certainly knew what plagiarism was. So why did I do it? I've spent many years trying to answer this question. While I am still processing all of this, I distinctly remember feeling like I could not ask for help when preparing the draft.

It wasn't that my professor wouldn't have helped me.

I just didn't feel like I could ask for it. *No, Angela, you can't ask for help, I thought. They'll find out who you really are. An imposter.*

I had only recently won The Best Paper Award in my Legal Writing section, and I felt like if I asked for help, particularly right before the draft was due, my teacher would: (a) know that I procrastinated and (b) think that I wasn't actually a good writer.

IMPOSTER SYNDROME

Have you ever felt like an imposter?

I had heard the phrase "imposter syndrome" before but didn't really know what it was. It wasn't until my editor, Hilary Jastram, brought it up during one of our conversations that I began thinking it could apply to me. I specifically remember writing a note to myself, "Look up Imposter Syndrome" during one of our calls.

Then I heard it again in other places. One of those places was on a podcast by Shawn Bolz (*Exploring the Marketplace Series*) that I regularly listen to. Bolz mentioned that many highly successful business leaders struggle or have struggled with imposter syndrome.

When I read about it, I'm pretty sure my jaw dropped.

Imposter syndrome "involves feelings of self-doubt and personal incompetence that persists despite your education, experience, and accomplishments."[34]

I have accomplished many great things in my life. A few of these accomplishments are listed below. The purpose of listing these is to help better paint a picture for you of how imposter syndrome has affected my life. I'm sure you have a similar list of your own that you can reference, and even though you may be proud of these achievements, you can still feel like an imposter in certain areas of your life. That's normal. I'm sharing

---

[34] https://www.healthline.com/health/mental-health/imposter-syndrome

some of the goals I've met with you so you can better understand the depths of my feelings.

In junior high school, I was the Valedictorian of my eighth-grade class. In high school, I played four sports (basketball, volleyball, softball, and track) and still graduated at the top of my class. Not the very top but up there. I won the state championship in the javelin throw in my senior year. I was a recipient of the National Scholar-Athlete Award, an award given to one graduating male and female student athlete.

I graduated college Cum Laude with a Bachelor of Arts degree in English.

Then, as you already know, I furthered my education by graduating with a Doctorate of Jurisprudence from law school.

None of these feats came easily. I was not born with a silver spoon in my mouth.

As a child, I felt like I was a slow learner and had to work extra hard to understand intellectual concepts. When I was younger, Mom and Dad put my twin sister and me through testing to see if we would qualify for the gifted program at a particular school. As it turns out, one of us qualified, but the other one didn't.

**They never told us which one didn't make it.
I always felt like it was me.**

It seemed it took me just a little bit longer to grasp knowledge. My parents may say otherwise, but because of my perceived failure and low self-image, I was convinced otherwise, and I had to work really hard to prove myself.

Partly because I didn't think I was good enough and partly because I always shot for perfection.

Attaining accolades is lovely, and I want you to hear what I'm saying. It's not attaining or achieving that was the issue. It was my mindset.

I was always striving for perfection, and anything less than that made me feel unworthy.

One of the challenges a person suffering from imposter syndrome deals with is anxiety about failing to replicate past successes.

I had won the Best Paper Award in my legal writing class only months before. Looking back, I can see it clearly. I held myself to such a high standard. I remember feeling immense anxiety and self-made pressure about replicating my past successes, especially in writing. Writing came the easiest out of everything I had done in my life. But I put an unnecessary burden on myself to write a perfect paper.

I didn't reach out to my professor for help in the drafting process when I should have.

Inner voices told me it would be weak to ask for help. That maybe I wasn't this great writer it appeared I was.

The truth is I didn't quite know what I was doing or the direction to take in the paper. With my English literature degree, I wanted to show my professor just how great and creative I could be.

Over Christmas break, we were to select the theme of our paper on the topic of "Fraud" and had been instructed to have our drafts ready early in the semester. I began researching what I could write about on and off for several weeks. After some time, I landed on something that seemed interesting—horse Fraud—specifically as it pertained to steroid use in horses. I spent the majority of my drafting time trying to figure out where to go with this topic. The night before the draft was due, I typed up 14 pages of notes from the reading that I had done with the intent and hope that a creative spark would ignite as I typed out all the words. By the time we were to submit our drafts, I still wasn't ready, so I took the 14 pages of notes and put a paper together. They were not my ideas. They were someone else's.

But I couldn't ask for help.

I could not ask for help.

Even now, as I think about why I did not ask for help and what the source of this fear was, a memory floats into my mind.

I was in high school, and it was late as I sat there and did my physics homework after dinner. With my demanding, year-round athletic schedule, my siblings and I had games or practice almost every school day. Nights were reserved for finishing up our studies.

Physics—not my cup of tea.

I remember working on a problem that I could not understand at all. It read like a foreign language, so I walked into the living room and asked my father for help. But I almost didn't want to because he was resting after work.

My father is a genius. He is a geophysicist and has a Ph.D. in physics, so I knew he would be able to help.

He walked into the room where I was doing my homework, assessed the problem I was working on, looked back at me, and said, matter-of-factly, "A monkey could do it." In the moment, the incompetency I was feeling heightened. I know my daddy would never intentionally hurt me. His love for me runs so deep! He would do anything to protect me.

Over the years, as I have thought about this moment, I now realize his intention was to tell me he believed in me so much, and knew how smart

I was, that he was trying to share his thoughts that I am not a monkey. But I was an overly sensitive teenager in full-blown angst, and immediately thought of the opposite: *I can't do this; therefore, I am dumber than a monkey.* Obviously, that is not true, and my dad has spent so much time with me proving how intelligent he believes me to be.

I allowed those words to make me feel small as I took them completely out of context.

And I suppose going forward, I never wanted to feel that way again.

When I submitted my draft of that paper in law school, I recall having a sense of relief that I could "check off" turning it in, but I had anxiety about the way it was done. Because I had typed all the notes on a separate Word document, it was as if I had forgotten which words were mine and which were someone else's. The only words that I knew were 100% mine were the words in the beautiful poem that I wrote at the front of the draft.

I wasn't careful, and I knew better.

I turned in the draft without citing the source of many of the ideas in the paper.

I took credit for others' words instead of creating my own.

I melted under the pressure and what resulted was self-sabotage.

I sabotaged my gift and tarnished my name.

After submitting the draft, I received a call from my professor to come in for a meeting, and my heart sank immediately. I knew what she wanted to meet about, and I stayed submerged in the depths of my self-made misery for a long time after that moment.

This was the beginning of a very long and tough journey.

I met with my professor and our honor court advisor in her office and admitted what I had done right away. I did not make excuses or try to justify it.

I admitted it.

AFTERMATH

In the wake of my honor code violation in law school, my professor graciously allowed me to rewrite a paper on a different topic. In that class, we also had to make a presentation on our paper, and I had already chosen to present first. After the plagiarism, my presentation was bumped to the end of the semester. My classmates must have known something had gone on, but they said nothing. Even in the face of that humiliation, I was determined to redeem myself in my professor's eyes and in my own.

But I was sinking.

I chose to write my second go-around dealing with adoption fraud. For the presentation, I wore a brown pixie wig, librarian glasses, and a suit. I also spoke with a British accent the entire time and put on this big show. Before our class started, the dean of the law school, who knew me, saw me outside the classroom. I was in character, wearing the outfit and speaking with an accent, and he had no idea who I was.

Nobody did.

I had a lot of fun that day. My professor later told me that I would have amjured the class (received the highest grade) if not for the violation.

While I had been offered redemption in this class, I was stripped of my title as honor court justice and was required to put in community service, which I did at the legal aid office near the law school. I also knew that I would likely have to sit before the Character and Fitness Committee of the Mississippi Bar after I graduated. It was a lot to take in.

I continued on in school, finishing out my time at Mississippi College School of Law with the word "plagiarist" hovering over my head. I allowed that word to define me for a time. But it wasn't the only thing that hovered over me.

As a Christian, I know that "we wrestle not against flesh and blood, but principalities, against powers, against rulers of the darkness of this world, against spiritual wickedness in high places." (Ephesians 6:12) During that season, I allowed the Enemy to get a foothold in other areas, too. I wasn't proud that I was being unfaithful in my marriage. Words like "adulterer" and "unworthy" also lingered over me, along with the onslaught of guilt, shame, and oppression.

I kept my shame and sadness hidden behind a smile.

And a bottle.

I thought that if I smiled enough, stuffed down the grief just far enough, and numbed myself to the pain, no one would have to know my misery. Life could go on as it should. As everyone expected it to.

But I just kept sinking lower.

My world seemed to fall apart just before graduation in the spring of 2011, as I had revealed my unfaithfulness to my husband at the time and was advised that I had to sit before the Character and Fitness Committee of the Mississippi Bar three days after graduation.

For many, graduation day is a time of celebration. But my heart was heavy … for a myriad of reasons … and it was difficult to smile.

But I did. Just like I had been doing.

The following Monday, I was sitting in front of the Character and Fitness Committee, with all eyes on me. I wore a robe of utter humiliation as they listened to me and prodded me with what seemed like endless questions, determining whether I had the requisite level of character to sit for the Mississippi Bar Exam.

Level of character? These words resounded in my head.

When did I not have character?

Didn't they know who I was?

I was the sweet, innocent, always-do-things-by-the-book girl.

How did this massive fall happen seemingly overnight?

But it didn't happen overnight. Somewhere along the way, I had allowed something or someone to enter in and grab a foothold.

And then I fell.

A local Mississippi attorney agreed to represent me before the Committee. Three professors from law school also agreed to be character witnesses for me. One of those professors was teaching a course in Mexico at the time and called into the hearing to testify on my behalf. He was the honor court advisor of Mississippi College School of Law. He was in the room when I admitted the violation to my professor.

One professor who agreed to testify on my behalf was the very professor whose trust I had broken in the writing class. She said at the hearing that she doesn't normally testify for students but wanted to for me.

She told the Committee on Admission to the Mississippi Bar that she trusted me and that I should be allowed to sit for the bar exam. I have the 119-page transcript of the hearing. Now and then, I return to her words: "The reason I offered [to testify] with Angela is that, if you're going to let anybody through, she's the one, okay? … And, for me, she is that linchpin, and I think that she is the kind that we rehabilitate…"

She called me the linchpin.

She called me *the one*.

NEW DIRECTIONS

After graduation and my hearing before the Mississippi Character and Fitness Committee, my husband and I separated, and I moved home to Louisiana.

It was a place where I felt safe and accepted.

In my childhood room at my parent's house, I immediately began studying for the Mississippi Bar Exam with high hopes that I could take it. A month or so into studying, I learned that my application was rejected by the Mississippi Board, even after the Character and Fitness Committee unanimously recommended that I sit for the Mississippi Bar Exam.

I was rejected and absolutely crushed.

Once again, I felt like a complete and utter failure. That day was one of the worst days. I'd sunk to the bottom of the ocean with weights strapped to my ankles as my failures floated to the surface—out in the open for everyone to see.

I shared with you about this day at the beginning of the book. I told you I bought a bottle of vodka after the crushing news came and slowly drove around a prominent neighborhood in our town. I just rolled along, drinking and hating myself.

Submerged in depression.

Thinking about how I had to go home and tell my parents what their little girl had done.

That was a heavy, dark time.

The waves were like shackles.

I didn't know what to do, where to turn, how to be—all I knew was that I had to get away.

So that I wouldn't have to face all the people who knew what happened.

So that I wouldn't have to see the disappointment on their faces.

I ran away to Colorado for work—a place I could escape to.

In a new world and with a new life, things had to get better. But I continued to numb the pain in my heart by filling myself with the pleasures of the world—men, booze, partying. I laughed my way through my days there.

But I had not healed.

I was only in hiding.

Because I had not healed—and because I had allowed the Enemy to steal my identity—I spent many nights in tears, with all the horrible thoughts about myself still suffocating me. All the words other people had said to me continued to steep in my soul like a hot cup of tea.

Except this tea was cold.

I could see people's faces and hear their words—the visions and sounds rotated in my mind like a record player on repeat when I tried to sleep at night. There was no escape from the agony I had brought on my life.

All I wanted to do was drift away.

CHAPTER 5

IDENTIFYING A PERSON LOST AT SEA

"The little cares that fretted me, I lost them yesterday
among the fields above the sea, among the winds at play."

—Elizabeth Barrett Browning

I know I am not the only person to have ever felt lost. It's probably more common than many even realize—seeing a person floating aimlessly through life, often suffering in silence. Ephesians 1:18 references the eyes of the heart. When you are lost, these eyes are glazed over, a sense of numbness infiltrates your being.

Lost at sea.

How did they arrive there? It wasn't overnight. A person arrived there because they:

- Drifted off course.

- Have no anchor to keep them in place.

- Have lost sight of the shore.

- Have forgotten who they are.

A PERSON LOST AT SEA HAS DRIFTED OFF COURSE.

In the sailing world, a ship can drift off course by a storm or unexpected winds that arise. The direction the captain had planned to take the ship is altered or delayed due to circumstances outside of his or her control.

Jennifer Appel and Tasha Fuiva were two such seafarers who were trapped on a storm-battered boat called the *Sea Nymph* in the middle of the Pacific Ocean for several months in 2017. They had left Honolulu, Hawaii on Appel's 50-foot vessel for what they expected to be an 18-day trip to Tahiti, followed by a few months of leisurely sailing in the South Pacific before returning home.

As they were leaving Hawaii, storm winds of 50 to 70 miles per hour battered their boat for three days, damaging their sails and mast. They did not learn the severity of the damage until a month later after another storm flooded their boat's engine. This is when they learned that the sails and mast could no longer generate enough wind power to keep the ship on course. They were eventually found by a Taiwanese fishing vessel after drifting aimlessly for almost six months. When found, they were thousands of miles in the wrong direction.[35]

In this case, the seafarers got off course because of a storm—something they had no control over. The ladies could have done nothing differently to prevent the storm from coming.

Sometimes a person gets lost at sea due to a storm in their life that arises unexpectedly. Maybe betrayal by someone they love or the sudden death of a loved one or relationship can cause an unexpected and unintentional drifting.

---

[35] https://thewest.com.au/news/world/women-lost-on-drifting-boat-in-pacific-ocean-for-months-tell-their-incredible-story-ng-b88643376z

A ship can also veer off course due to a series of decisions, actions, or lack thereof within a seafarer's control.

On July 18, 2018, a Netherlands-registered cargo vessel called *MV Priscilla* was traveling from Europe to England carrying 3,300 tons of fertilizer when it ran aground off Orkney in the Northern Isles of Scotland. An investigation found that the watchman on board in charge of keeping the boat on a certain path was viewing music videos on his phone, so he wasn't paying attention to the ship's direction. Before he had time to correct the path of the ship, it ran aground on rocks.[36]

In this case, the ship drifted off course due to decisions made by the vessel's watchman. When the watchman realized the ship was not where it was supposed to be, he relied solely on radar data to steer the ship between the two small islands he could see ahead. But there was a problem looming that he could have avoided. The navigational information would have shown him that there was a shallow reef between the islands.

Instead of getting back on the planned route, he chose an alternate plan of attack that put the ship in imminent danger.

Like this watchman, a person adrift in their life can get that way due to a series of decisions preventing them from staying on their targeted path. Notice I've described this as a "series" and not as just one decision or event that causes them to drift.

A person lost at sea may also find themselves miles from their intended destination because they have no anchor.

---

[36] https://www.itv.com/news/2019-10-03/grounded-ship-drifted-off-course-while-officer-viewed-music-videos-report-finds

Once a ship makes it to its place of destination, the captain or crew will throw out the anchor. The anchor is a vital piece of a ship's equipment and is the reason a boat will not float away.

My husband and I enjoy sailing. One year, we were sailing north of Fort Pickens in Pensacola, Florida, with our family and children. We had anchored just offshore to explore the beach.

While on shore, we looked out into the Gulf and noticed ominous gray clouds getting closer. A storm had popped up out of nowhere. We rushed back to the boat as lightning struck around us!

Please, God, protect us! I prayed, looking back to make sure the girls were okay.

I know they were frightened.

We made it back to the boat as the pelting rain fell, hurriedly climbed aboard, went below deck, and closed all the windows. We could not see where we were, but at least we were inside and safe from the lightning storm. A short time later, my husband heard a sound coming from the front of the boat. It sounded like a bucket full of large rocks had dropped into the water from the deck above us. When he went up on deck to see where the sound came from, he noticed we had drifted.

The reason?

We had lost our anchor.

The sound my husband had heard from below deck was the anchor untying from the boat. He found it, but if he hadn't, we would have floated aimlessly during the storm.

Every person needs an anchor. I don't care how strong you think you are—if you don't have an anchor keeping you in place, you will drift.

Our anchor is Jesus Christ. He keeps us resting firm and secure. When we keep him as an anchor for our souls, we will not get tossed about.

Below the surface of any calm water lies the potential for an undercurrent to take you downstream—generally not toward Jesus but away from him. When you drift, it's normally not toward what will make you better.

If you leave a ship in the middle of the open sea or gulf, no matter how calm the water may seem on the surface, it will eventually move. Without an anchor keeping it securely in place, the ship is destined for waters where you never intended it to go.

But you can learn to be alert to the changes of drifting before you move too far in the wrong direction.

**Before you notice the outward drifting,
an inward drifting occurs.**

You will notice someone who has drifted because what is happening on the inside of someone generally overflows to the outside, whether it is good or bad.

Luke 6:45 says, "For the mouth speaks what the heart is full of." Meaning what is on the inside will come out and be seen on the outside. For a person drifting inwardly due to a series of choices they are making, subtle changes in their behavior may alert you that something is not quite right.

You'll see their red flag rippling in the wind.

Listen to this inward warning.

For example, you may think that someone who posts nothing but selfies on social media is all about other people. Wrong! They incessantly post pictures of themselves because they want other people to see them.

They are all about themselves.

And someone who is all about themselves tends to put their wants and desires in front of others' needs. Many times, the line between right and wrong can become distorted to them.

I'm not saying that posting a selfie on social media means you are drifting but it does show where your focus is.

You.

I speak from experience. During my season in Colorado, I took way too many pictures of myself with my phone for other people to see.

I was in a season of drifting, but I didn't have the eyes to see it. I made many justifications in my behavior based on what felt good to me in the moment, including inappropriate behavior I was normalizing in my life and boundaries I was crossing.

There are so many things I am still learning about myself from that time. What I do know to be true is that I had lost the anchor to my soul. That anchor is Jesus Christ.

I relied on myself—what I felt was right at the time. That, my friends, is a very dangerous mindset.

A person lost at sea has lost sight of the shore.

When a person is lost at sea, their visibility over distance is limited. Isaiah 44:18 says, "They do not know, nor do they discern, for He has shut their eyes, so that they cannot see, and their hearts, so that they cannot understand."

Most of the time, a person cannot see the shore because the lens through which they view life needs to be cleaned or even replaced.

The shore in a person's life is their destiny.

When you lose sight of shore, you may not know that you could be mere feet from the place you desire to be. You could be so close to a break-through, but when you cannot see how close you are to your destiny or destination, giving up seems an easier choice than pushing forward.

A person who has lost sight of shore has allowed the waves to pull them out. These can be waves of depression or torment that take them further from their destiny.

When I knew I was drifting, I allowed the waves of torment and depression to take me.

I actually believed I deserved both.

I remember many nights lying in my bed and feeling demonic spirits holding me down in my bed. Tormenting me. I was terrified of the night, and I knew I had opened the door to allow them to stay due to choices I had made in my life and marriage. Just as an imposter can access your confidential data if you let them, the same happens when you allow the devil access to your life through an open door.

Because I thought I deserved both torment and depression, I allowed these demons to stay much longer than they should have. I hated it, but I didn't know life could be different, and I certainly didn't know how to make it different. I let the oppression take me further into my depression while losing sight of what was important to me.

Like integrity, relationships, and honor.

What I saw instead was a hazy mist in front of my life, causing the shore—where my destiny was waiting patiently for me—to seem further and further away.

A person lost at sea has forgotten who they are.

A person lost at sea has lost their identity and forgotten they were made for rough waters.

They can no longer see the light they carry.

They can no longer see that their light shines from within.

They no longer remember their destiny does not involve floating aimlessly in the water.

Their destiny is on the shore.

In a scene from *The Lion King*, Simba slowly walks up to a watering hole and peers inside. He is looking for his father but only sees his reflection staring back at him. Rafiki, a mandrill, touches the water, and the waves change Simba's reflection into his father, Mufasa. I love the ensuing dialogue.

Rafiki says, "You see? He lives in you."

Mufasa then appears as a partially formed spirit in the sky and says his son's name—"Simba."

Simba: Father?

Mufasa: Simba, you have forgotten me.

Simba: No. How could I?

Mufasa: You have forgotten who you are and so have forgotten me. Look inside yourself, Simba. You are more than what you have become....

Simba: How can I go back? I'm not who I used to be.

Mufasa: [Now a fully formed presence]: Remember who you are. You are my son and the one true king. Remember who you are.

Simba: [Mufasa's spirit begins to disappear] No! Please don't! Please don't leave me!

Mufasa: Remember.

Simba: Father!

Mufasa: Remember.

Simba: Don't leave me!

Mufasa: Remember.

This is such a powerful scene, and so many of us can relate to it. When we lose our footing, we feel like we are walking alone. That we cannot go back or face certain people in our lives because of our choices.

Is this you?

Have you forgotten who you are?

Look inside yourself. You are brave. You are courageous. You are more than a conqueror!

You are more than what you have become.

Identity can be defined as "who you are, the way you think about yourself, the way you are viewed by the world, and the characteristics that define you."[37]

---

[37] https://www.yourdictionary.com/identity

As a child of God, your identity is in Christ. This is your inheritance. Your worth and your value is not measured by your performance, credentials, financial status, or career. It is measured by who you are.

1 Peter 2:9 says, "you are a chosen people, a royal priesthood, a holy nation, God's special possession, that you may declare the praises of Him who called you out of darkness into His wonderful light."

IDENTITY THEFT

A person lost at sea has not only lost their identity, but it has also been stolen from them.

John 10:10 says, "The thief comes only to steal and kill and destroy; I have come that they may have life, and have it to the full."

Identity theft is nothing new. News reports relay the latest breaches of security in our personal and professional lives; the data for millions of people is regularly stolen. Firewalls get hacked, passwords stolen, and confidential information is passed into the hands of criminals.

When a person loses their identity, they can easily be tossed about. They can easily get pulled under by the rough waters of life. Worse, they can forget they are not alone in the boat they're struggling to steer.

Isaiah 43:2 says, "When you go through deep waters, I will be with you. When you go through rivers of difficulty, you will not drown."

This is a promise.

When someone's identity is stolen, their private information has been taken without their permission. It muddles truth and they are unable to see it or their purpose clearly.

I had a very powerful dream a few years ago about identity theft as well as a powerful strategy to combat it.

In this dream, I was at a university with a few other people when an online imposter emailed me trying to get me to click on a link so he could access personal information.

I noticed this person was an imposter pretty easily.

Because I had eyes to see it.

I had the ability to be aware of his schemes.

The imposter was pretending to be someone else. He was emailing from the "U.S. Benk" instead of "Bank." Seeing the word "Bank" misspelled put me on notice.

It raised a red flag.

I did not click on the link. I did not allow the imposter to steal my identity or anyone else's. A woman was standing next to me, and I was telling her all about what the imposter was trying to do. To our right, inside the room we were in, was a man in a suit sitting at a desk. He had been listening to my conversation with the woman about the imposter.

I felt like this man ran the school.

He looked at me and asked, "Do you know what time it is?"

I glanced down at the digital clock on his desk and saw in red letters *11:02*. It was 11:02 pm in the dream.

I told him what I saw: "11:02." He said that over the next two hours, three people would be hit with thoughts of committing suicide. These three people were students at the school. As soon as I heard him speak of this, I began praying for them out loud.

And then I began saying, "Fill them up! Fill them up! Fill them up!" over and over and over until I was practically screaming it. As I prayed for these people, I could literally feel something happening inside me. There was an electric current inside my body—as if I could feel what was happening to those people. It was like as they were filled with the Holy Spirit, the voice of the enemy was muffled.

I woke up from the dream, continuing to pray for those three people. Continuing to declare, "Fill them up! Fill them up! Fill them up!" Then I felt the same electric current—the very one I felt in the dream!

What I learned from this dream: Prayer is a strategy of protection.

Being filled with the Holy Spirit is also a strategy of protection.

This is protection from our adversary, the Devil, who, according to 1 Peter 5:8, "prowls around like a roaring lion, seeking someone to devour." We must protect our identity from this imposter who wants nothing more than to take it from us. Without protection, suicidal thoughts can pierce the heart, causing a person to take action instead of letting those thoughts bounce off their armor.

The Devil wants to bring death, but God wants to bring abundant life. He wants our life to be full. When we are filled with His spirit, we will remember who we are!

Are you lost at sea?

Have you drifted off course?

Have you lost your anchor?

Have you lost sight of the shore?

Have you forgotten who you are?

If your answer is "Yes," my prayer for you is the same as my prayer for the three people fighting for their lives in my dream:

Fill them up!

Fill them up!

Fill them up!

In the filling, may you remember who you are. May you regain what was lost.

Once you do, you can help others who are lost.

Lost people are all around us. They are hurting yet try so hard to keep the fact they are lost hidden from the world. But if you look closely enough, you can discern who is lost and who has been found. Both could easily be standing on either side of you in the grocery store, in your office, in your family, or even in the mirror.

Keep a watchful eye. When you spot a lost soul, reach out to them.

Don't give them a condemning glance.

You know what it's like to be them.

See them through the lens of love and help bring them back home.

CHAPTER 6

FOUND AT SEA

"A setback only paves the way for a comeback."

—Evander Holyfield

"Okay, you can do this," I told myself, on deck to throw the javelin in my very first track meet ever. I was a junior in high school.

Nothing to worry about … except for the hundreds of eyes staring at you, ready to see the spear fly.

When I heard my name called, I tried to put on my confident face and get in my stance. I started counting the steps in my head as I sprinted down the runway—*one, two, three…* When I got to *eight*, I planted my left foot, arched my back, and launched the javelin. As I followed through with my body, I felt a sudden and excruciating pain in my back. I glanced up to see how far the javelin had gone and saw it somersaulting through the air, landing just yards from where it started. I then realized I had hit my back *with* the javelin as I came forward to throw.

Many people saw it. Too many!

I wanted to hide. Forever.

But did I? No. My parents taught me better than that. I absorbed the embarrassing and completely humiliating moment—and I moved on.

I kept practicing and perfecting my technique throughout the rest of the track season. I got all the way to the regional meet that year but knew that my senior year was the year for gold.

And it was.

My dad once told me that to master something, one must become a student of the art. I did that my senior year by studying javelin videos and literature about proper throwing mechanics but, most importantly, by practicing. My dad, sisters, and I would spend hours after church on Sundays fine-tuning and getting down the correct form at a high school near our house.

MASTERING THE ART

I came in first place in the javelin at almost every track meet my senior year and set several meet records. I ended the year by winning the state championship at Louisiana State University and being the LHSAA (Louisiana High School Athletic Association) 2A State Javelin Champion.

I still feel an immense sense of accomplishment when I think about the road that led me there.

It wasn't easy to trek. Getting there took hard work, sacrifice, passion, and dedication.

Failure was not an option.

I had fallen, yes. But I wasn't going to stay down. Do you see the difference?

Falling is inevitable. It's only failure when you don't get back up.

I learned an invaluable lesson through that experience—one I would need years later:

Don't let a failing moment keep you on the ground.
Those moments are merely stepping stones to your success.

Or, as Pastor Dharius Morshun Daniels aptly says, "Failure doesn't have to be fatal. It's a prison or a school. You get to choose."

I am not new to a failing moment. I've had plenty of them. Sometimes it's taken me longer to get up after falling, but I always do. I have that power. You have that power. It's part of the light inside us—it enables us to try again, stand up in the face of disappointment, look rejection in the eye, and say, "Today is your last day."

When I ran away to Colorado, I often wept burning hot tears that seemed to come from my very core. They scorched my cheeks from the despair and pain I felt for myself and the people I had hurt. I tried to turn off my feelings—as if there was an invisible button I could push to do it—so it wouldn't hurt as much. But that didn't last long. I learned that I was only damaging myself further by not confronting or dealing with the pain.

When I eventually moved home, I felt the delicate pull of God in my life. His quiet whispers to my spirit. He was pursuing me, although I didn't acknowledge it at first. I was divorced and still wading through the waters of disappointment. This included the continual layering on of ungodly beliefs and others' harsh words in my mind.

WORDS HURT

On a day that stands out in my mind, I was visiting my brother and his wife at their friends' house. I had not seen their friend in some time. When I walked through the door where a group was visiting, my brother's friend looked at me and asked, "Are you Rebecca?" Rebecca is my younger sister.

I don't recall exactly how I replied, but I let him know I was not her. All I remember are the following biting words that pierced my heart:

"Oh, you're the whore."

I was silent and immediately looked down in embarrassment.

The room got quiet.

My brother looked at me.

I didn't know how to respond and was so taken aback that this person could be so bold. What he said hurt deeply, but I did not break down and cry when his words came out.

In that moment, I believed what he said and thought I deserved that quick punch in the gut. In short, I'd come into agreement with that ungodly belief.

For a while.

The Enemy had stolen my identity and replaced it with an ugly, false view of myself.

I got to the point where I would cringe internally when someone said, "Oh, you're an attorney?" Inwardly I would respond, "Yes, I have my degree, but I cannot practice. All that work for nothing. What a waste."

Outwardly, I would quietly smile.

I hated that it had become this way. I had fought so hard for three years to be an attorney, and it all seemed for nothing.

And on top of that, I had a failed marriage.

Oh, the stench of sin.

I hated what I had done and my connection to it. Because of what happened, I could not walk around with confidence. Instead, I walked around with unforgiveness marinating in my heart and let my failures dictate my present circumstance.

MY COMEBACK

Then I decided that my failures did not define me—that all those words, the unworthiness I felt—just wasn't true.

Instead of allowing my failures to swallow me whole, I was determined to pursue a comeback.

This meant facing my fear.

Them—the legal community that had rejected me.

I would come face to face once more with the gaping failures I had endured during law school. As you know, these were part of the reason I had rejected myself.

It was a big, scary step to take because it meant I had to open the wound again. I had to let it rise to the surface and sit there exposed.

But as it sat there exposed and my failings rose and became visible for all to see, I began to rise with them.

Slowly, subtly, but surely.

I applied for the Louisiana Bar Exam, which required me to explain my law school honor code violation on the application. It hurt, but it was necessary.

The Louisiana Bar Exam takes place over three full days and a period of one business week. It is given two times a year, in February and July.

I had applied for the February exam that year and was very concerned that Louisiana would reject me as Mississippi had by not allowing me to sit for the bar exam. After submitting the application, the Louisiana Committee on Bar Admissions (LASCBA) advised that I would not find out if I could sit until approximately 30 days before the exam.

I kept a close eye on my calendar and mailbox.

When the 30-day mark came and went, I became anxious because I hadn't yet received approval. My mind began traveling down a dark, pessimistic road.

Before I fully surrendered to it, I reached out to the Administrator for the LASCBA for an update. This was on a Monday.

An hour after I reached out to her, she responded that my approval letter had been mailed that previous Friday.

Approval letter.

Approval!

I raced down to my mailbox and found the letter. I had not been rejected.

I shifted my focus to studying as much as I could for the Louisiana bar exam while working as a landman in various clerk of court offices, where I researched land records in the oil and gas industry. It was a lot to handle, but I was determined to have my comeback.

The Louisiana bar exam was held at the Pontchartrain Convention and Civic Center in New Orleans, Louisiana. Since testing took place every other day, I made the two-and-a-half-hour drive to and from New Orleans the week of testing. I didn't have extra funds to stay at a hotel the entire week.

The week of testing was fierce.

On Monday, we tested all day.

Tuesday, we were given the day to prepare for the next day of testing.

Wednesday came and went, and I was relieved to have only one more day of testing.

Friday came, and we knew we were almost to the finish line.

When I crossed the finish line on Friday afternoon, I felt relieved but also anxious because, on one of the testing days, my personal computer that I'd brought for testing had a glitch. I'd been unable to complete a portion of one test. I hoped my performance on the others was enough to carry me through.

I didn't know anyone else who was taking the exam, and I was just fine with that. This allowed me to watch others and listen to their conversations when we were in the lobby outside the testing room. I overheard many people say this was their second or third time taking the exam. One woman said it was her fifth time attempting to pass!

Please, Lord, help me pass it the first time.

I had to wait a few months for the exams to be reviewed.

On the day results were posted, I didn't want to look right away. I *needed* to pass. After all I had been through—after developing the courage to try again—it *had to* go my way.

I logged into my portal, knowing the minimum score I needed to pass.

650.

650 out of 900.

When my eyes rested on my score, my heart deflated because I was only a few points shy of passing.

I sighed.

And cried.

You're not good enough rang in my head.

Along with *I really am a failure.*

I carried these thoughts for several weeks.

The inner voices of discouragement telling me my trying was over.

And then...

And then...

I heard another voice.

But this time it was in my heart.

Get up.

Get up.

Get up and try again.

You did not come this far to give up.

You are a champion.

You are my champion.

So, I stood up, gathered myself off the floor, and I tried again.

I reapplied for the July Louisiana bar exam, paying the hefty $875 application fee—knowing that I barely had the money in my account to pay for the application. But I did it anyway—on faith that things would be different this time.

And I went into battle.

I took a five-week hiatus from work and spent over 12 hours every single day for five weeks preparing for the July Louisiana bar exam.

I took every practice test for each bar exam subject from the last several years, hand-wrote definitions and acronyms on thousands of notecards front and back and memorized countless concepts. I also created a Memory Palace (a study method that helps people remember large chunks of information by associating a familiar place with mnemonic images) to store the immense volume of information I was putting in my brain.

Needless to say, after five weeks—

I.

Was.

Ready.

I also bought a new computer so there would be no technological issues. And during the week of the examination, I stayed at a family friend's house on the grounds of the New Orleans Baptist Theological Seminary instead of driving hours back and forth between testing days. My nerves were calmer than last time because I knew what the experience would be like.

Now, I was full of knowledge!

I remember walking into the Ponchartrain Convention and Civic Center with confidence.

After each of the nine exams, I knew I had done well.

But would it be enough?

On October 11th of that year, which just so happened to be the 12th anniversary of my Granny's funeral (she was the first person close to me to have graduated to Heaven), I found out that it was enough.

I had passed!

BUT WAIT...

That same day, I also received a letter from the LASCBA saying it denied my license due to circumstances surrounding the Mississippi Bar Admission denial.

I was again crushed.

And somewhat angry. *How could you take my money twice, let me sit for the bar exam twice, and now tell me it's not enough?*

But I did not wallow in disappointment.

Instead, determined, I hired an attorney recommended to assist with these kinds of matters.

The 40-minute drive to his office was difficult for my heart. After all the ups and downs I had experienced the last few years, and particularly in the recent months, I knew when I arrived at his office that I would have to explain again what had happened.

And it still hurt!

I didn't know what kind of man he would be. Would he be compassionate, or would he view me like a prisoner trying to appeal a prison sentence?

I walked into his office, my heart fluttering. His daughter, who also worked with him, was there, too.

I sat in a chair opposite his desk, law books all around. I couldn't tell how I would feel until...

A soft smile crossed his face.

That relaxed me and simultaneously resurrected in me the idea that I wasn't the horrible person I thought I was or had been made to feel.

He listened to my story.

At the end of our time together, he told me he wanted to help me.

Together, he, his daughter, their team, and I worked on a Petition for Admission to the Louisiana Supreme Court. Since funds were tight on my end, they said it would be most cost-effective if I drafted the petition, and they assisted in finalizing it before submission. They gave me a template to use, and I got to work.

Once the petition was drafted, we spent the next few weeks gathering exhibits and finalizing the petition for submission.

We submitted the petition in November, knowing it could be up to 60 days before we heard a response.

I waited.

I had become good at waiting.

Nearly 60 days later, the waiting was over. On this day, I was granted admission to practice law in the State of Louisiana.

They said, "Yes."

At that moment, the heavy burden of rejection, disappointment, and failure I had carried for so long lifted off me, and healing began.

NOW

Today, I am remarried and living an abundant life—one that is full of joy. My husband and I have four beautiful girls, Cannon Patton (twenty-one), Priya Rose Lalande (six years old), Ayla Reine Lalande (four years old), and Cira Lassen Lalande (two years old).

I own a title company offering title insurance, escrow, and closing services for residential and commercial properties in Louisiana.

I am an attorney—a title I didn't know I would ever be able to say with confidence. Ever.

I am forgiven, cherished, loved, and whole. I no longer carry the shame, guilt, oppression, and rejection that had attached themselves to me for years.

Morning came. It always does.
Night can only tarry for so long.

YOUR NIGHT

You might have picked up this book because you are living in a night season. Or you're coming up on one.

You feel alone, unworthy, dirty, defiled.

Maybe you are on the path to sitting in front of a Character and Fitness Committee just as I did or have begun embarking down a similarly dark road. I hope my words—my story, my testimony—may prevent you from having to walk the same path.

If you are walking toward the ledge or standing at the ledge, dipping your toes in waters you do not need to touch or even be near, I want you to know that what you think is waiting for you on the other side is not worth it.

Your perception might be that this route will lead you to gain the world, the golden ring you think will make you happy in the moment. But when strived for in the wrong manner, what you are giving up for what you are gaining is not worth it.

Mark 8:35 says, "For whosoever will save his life shall lose it; but whosoever shall lose his life for my sake and the gospel's, the same shall save it. For what shall it profit a man if he shall gain the whole world, and lose his own soul?"

Look around you and within you—if you have the choice to take the high road or the low road in any situation, always take the high road. It is the right road. Taking the right road will save you much pain and heartache.

If you've already taken the low road, whatever that road looks like for you, know there is always a chance for redemption. You can always find a spot to turn around. Don't hide from the people who love you the most, and don't think for one minute that God is not with you. You have His DNA! You are His child, and He will love you even when you don't love yourself. He sees you not as you see yourself. In this state, you see yourself broken and battered, but He sees you whole. When you take in this truth, it will set you free.

HOW TO BE AN OVERCOMER

After my law school failures, I stepped onto the boat of depression and drifted out to sea.

I eventually found the light—and found my way back to shore.

Back to the land of the living.

Along the way, I learned three invaluable truths that have helped me in almost every area of my life. Understanding them has helped shape my perspective and mindset as I discovered how to be an overcomer.

These truths are:

- You are perfectly imperfect.
- Your setback births your comeback.
- Your giant (whatever's in your way) is smaller than you think.

YOU ARE PERFECTLY IMPERFECT.

I've never met a person who has never made a mistake, and I know I never will. Making mistakes is part of our humanity, but so is rising from them. I also never met a champion who achieved that rank immediately. It took time and hard work.

You must let go of the perfectionist mindset.

Allow yourself to make mistakes, and when you do, if you learn from those mistakes, you will grow.

YOUR SETBACK BIRTHS YOUR COMEBACK.

We generally see a setback as failure. I sure did. I have had setback after setback after setback in my life. These moments chipped away at my soul. From my embarrassing first track meet throwing the javelin to being rejected as an attorney, I had every excuse in the world to give up. Maybe you feel like that now, too.

Without these setbacks, I would not have had a comeback. I would not have known the gift that can come out of pain. I would not have known the resiliency inside me.

J.K. Rowling once said in a Harvard commencement address:

"It is impossible to live without failing at something unless you live so cautiously that you might as well not have lived at all—in which case, you fail by default… Failure taught me things about myself that I could have learned no other way. I discovered that I had a strong will and more discipline than I had suspected; I also found out that I had friends whose value was truly above the price of rubies.

"The knowledge that you have emerged wiser and stronger from setbacks means that you are, ever after, secure in your ability to survive. You will never truly know yourself, or the strength of your relationships until both have been tested by adversity. Such knowledge is a true gift, for all that it is painfully won, and it has been worth more than any qualification I ever earned."

YOUR GIANT IS SMALLER THAN YOU THINK.

Fear can make our obstacles seem so big! Facing the legal community after my initial Mississippi rejection was hard.

The fear of failing again was practically debilitating!

Just thinking about the prospect of failing again or being rejected again made me almost not try again. That's what fear does. It prevents us from moving forward.

But if I had given into fear, if I had given into the idea that this giant was too big for me, then I never would have seen the victory on the other side.

In his book, *The Obstacle is The Way*, Ryan Holiday says, "All great victories … involved resolving vexing problems with a potent cocktail of creativity, focus and daring. When you have a goal, obstacles are actually teaching you how to get where you want to go—carving you a path." Further, that "obstacles are actually opportunities to test ourselves, to try new things, and, ultimately, to triumph."

If you have a setback or obstacle in your path that seems too big,

Remember …

Your giant is smaller than you think. It's all about how you perceive the obstacle in your way.

Many times, the obstacle in your way is there to teach you.

MY PROMISE TO YOU

If you take these truths to heart—

If you let them marinate in your innermost being—

If you will apply them to your life—

You will be an overcomer.

You will rise again.

You will come back to the land of the living.

I am living proof that you can breathe again.

You *will* breathe again.

You will be found.

When you're found,

You will no longer be drifting,

You will find the shore,

And you will remember who you are.

CHAPTER 7

BECOMING A PRISM

"Let the world burn through you.
Throw the prism light, white hot, on paper."

—Ray Bradbury

Becoming a prism is the most vital step in The Lighthouse Method. While all the steps are important, this one is the crux of it all. If you cannot become a prism, your journey to the light is impossible.

Why?

Because light cannot travel through an object that is not transparent, having been purified to become a conduit for light. You must become like a prism to shine again—so light cannot only shine in you but through you. The same is true of any person looking to heal and desperately wanting to shine again.

Materials that form a prism must go through a purification process to become a beautiful, sustaining creation.

We must also be purified for our light to pierce the night.
Remember, to become a prism, you must be purified.

THE PURIFICATION STEPS

To "purify" means to "remove contaminants from."[38] The purification process starts with understanding how glass is made. As I mentioned earlier, glass is formed by combining sand, soda ash, and limestone and melting them at a very high temperature. Before being purified, a less-than-appealing object made of these three raw materials exists. When this object is put under fire, however, the impurities melt away, and a prism is formed.

Isn't that amazing?!

The same happens to us when we go through our purification process. When we are cleansed—when all our dirt is washed away—we have clarity and can see and be seen differently. Our cleansing takes place from the inside out. It starts on the inside and overflows to the exterior.

As a reminder, the Five Purification Steps are:

1. **Humility**

2. **Confession**

3. **Repentance**

4. **Forgiveness**

5. **Replacement**

How then do you start your own purification process to become a prism?

1. HUMILITY
....

The first step is to go low. Submerge yourself in humility. This involves being honest with yourself and the situation. It means taking ownership of what happened or what was done, and it postures you for healing.

---

[38] https://www.lexico.com/en/definition/purify

For example, you may have made a bad decision. Perhaps you have broken someone's trust. Maybe you had an affair.

You could play the blame game all day long. Many people do, which is why reconciliation doesn't happen. But at some point, you must look inside yourself. This is called introspection, and it means reflecting on your part in what happened and taking ownership of it.

Your spouse's lack of intimacy with you didn't make you do what you did. Their constant disrespect of you, if that's what it was, didn't cause you to run into someone else's arms.

Ultimately, you made the choice to cross the boundary.

The Way Up is Down

When you go low, you are lifted up.

James 4:6-10 says, "God opposes the proud but shows favor to the humble. Submit yourselves, then, to God. Resist the devil, and he will flee from you. Come near to God, and he will come near to you. Wash your hands, you sinners, and purify your hearts, you double-minded. Grieve, mourn and wail. Change your laughter to mourning and your joy to gloom. Humble yourselves before the Lord, and he will lift you up."

Pride is one of Satan's chief weapons in his warfare against God's people.

God wants us to be humble.

Satan wants us to be proud.

Light versus dark.

This has always been the battle.

In humility, you empty yourself.

You lay down pride.

You must, or you will fall.

As Proverbs 16:18 says, "Pride goes before destruction, a haughty spirit before a fall."

In this step, your heart posture says, "I was wrong, and I want to make it right."

Your humility will lift you up, but you must first go low to get there.

The way up is down.

2. CONFESSION

While you are postured in this way, you must confess, for confession is the doorway to your cleansing.

1 John 1:9 says, "If we confess our sins, He is faithful and just and will forgive us our sins and purify us from all unrighteousness."

Confession can be difficult when your ego stands in the way, demanding your silence. You don't want to speak of what you did or what was done to you because you feel like if the words escaped your lips, shame would fall like a tsunami, and you would drown under the weight of the remembrance of it.

You will not drown. That is a lie you tell yourself.

No, you will rise above the waves.

When you speak the words, admitting your fault, pride begins to fall, your selfishness is removed, and you are one step closer to purification.

The Power in Your Words

There is power in the words you speak.

Proverbs 18:21 says, "Life and death are in the power of the tongue, and those who love it will eat its fruit."

Your words can be life-giving or destructive.

If you're over the age of three, you understand the destruction that words can bring. Words can hurt.

Maybe your best friend told you she no longer wanted to be your friend.

Maybe your boss told you that you just weren't cutting it at work, and they had to let you go.

Maybe an ex-boyfriend or girlfriend told you they were interested in someone else and that you weren't pretty or handsome enough for them.

Those words hurt.

I have received hurtful words, and I have also given them. Particularly when I had so much hate toward myself inside… I've said plenty of things I wish I could take back. To friends. To family members. To the air about friends or family members.

But I can't.

What I can do is confess and repent from saying those words.

I can speak blessings over those people instead.

Yes, there is power in your words.

Your words carry the ability to set things in motion. I believe the intentions we speak into the world go to work in our real lives, including angels being put on assignment as a result of our prayers. Words allow us to pull possibilities across the veil. We don't realize it, but we have more authority than we know, and our words can create miracles.

Confession can take place in any setting. You do not need to be before a priest or pastor. You can be by yourself under the open heavens in your backyard or under the light of your bedroom. You can be driving. You can be walking. You can be doing a lot of things, but you must get the words out of your heart and mouth.

Psalm 32: 5 says, "Then I acknowledged my sin to you and did not cover up my iniquity. I said, 'I will confess my transgressions to the Lord.' And you forgave the guilt of my sin."

What keeps you moving through the door to cleansing is what is happening in your heart.

You must have your heart in it!

Confession without repentance leaves the confessor standing on the threshold of change without the opportunity to walk into it fully.

---

3. REPENTANCE
....

Repentance involves a change of heart and direction. The Greek word "repentance" translated from the Bible means "to change one's way of life as the result of a complete change of thought and attitude with regard to sin and righteousness."[39]

---

[39] Greek-English Lexicon of the New Testament Based on Semantic Domains, J.P. Louw and Eugene Nida, 1988). https://lifehopeandtruth.com/change/repentance/what-is-repentance/.

When you reach true repentance, you have accepted responsibility for your actions. You then turn your heart and mind around, living with the complete resolve to never go that way again.

In the turning, you can now repair what was broken.

I remember the first time I saw the timeless musical *Les Miserables*. I was a junior in college, studying abroad for a semester in London, England. The storyline, the lyrics … touched so deeply. I fell in love with it then.

But it wasn't until I grew older that I truly appreciated the message. Jean Valjean's story is one of redemption. He was given a second chance at life after serving many years in prison for stealing bread to feed his sister's children during an economic depression.

In one scene, particularly in the 2012 version where Hugh Jackman plays Jean Valjean, we can see him reach true repentance. After his release from prison, Valjean stole silver from Bishop Myriel. When he was caught by the police, the Bishop showed him grace and allowed him to keep the silver, and even gave him more for his journey.

This moment of grace wrecked Valjean. He realized what he had done and changed his life from that point forward.

Valjean's Soliloquy by Hugh Jackman shows the moment of his change, and I want you to read his powerful words:

> What have I done?
> Sweet Jesus, what have I done?
> Become a thief in the night
> Become a dog on the run
> Have I fallen so far
> And is the hour so late
> That nothing remains but the cry of my hate
> The cries in the dark that nobody hears
> Here where I stand at the turning of the years?

If there's another way to go
I missed it 20 long years ago
My life was a war that could never be won
They gave me a number and murdered Valjean
When they chained me and left me for dead
Just for stealing a mouthful of bread

Yet why did I allow that man
To touch my soul and teach me love?
He treated me like any other
He gave me his trust
He called me brother
My life he claims for God above
Can such things be?
For I had come to hate the world
This world that always hated me

Take an eye for an eye
Turn your heart into stone
This is all I have lived for
This is all I have known

One word from him and I'd be back
Beneath the lash, upon the rack
Instead he offers me my freedom
I feel my shame inside me like a knife
He told me that I have a soul
How does he know?
What spirit comes to move my life?
Is there another way to go?

I am reaching, but I fall
And the night is closing in
As I stare into the void
To the whirlpool of my sin
I'll escape now from that world
From the world of Jean Valjean
Jean Valjean is nothing now
Another story must begin

Jean Valjean experienced a moment of grace and became a changed man.

A transformed leader.

A leader who loved.

A leader who chose forgiveness with no conditions.

All of it stemmed from his repentance after receiving grace.

4. FORGIVENESS

Both Heaven and Hell heard you when you muttered these words while hot tears rolled down your cheeks, staining them:

"I will never forgive myself."

I've said those words many times.

Out loud.

And I meant them.

I vowed never to forgive myself for my affair. I vowed never to forgive myself for the plagiarism. I vowed never to forgive myself for the mess I had made of my life because I felt like I did not deserve forgiveness!

Each time I said those words, it was as if I unknowingly clasped an iron-clad prison chain around my ankles.

Remember, your words matter.

You set your fate in the words you speak. You also set your fate in the words you don't.

Sometimes the hardest person to forgive is yourself, but you must forgive yourself if you truly want to be set free.

Lewis B. Smedes once said, "To forgive is to set a prisoner free and discover that the prisoner was you."

I completely agree.

Forgiveness is a release from your prison. You have to take the key out of your pocket to let yourself out of your cell.

Effects of Unforgiveness

Not forgiving yourself or another can affect you negatively physically and spiritually.

Various studies have been carried out to show that this can lead to anxiety and depression, which can be seen in the following health issues:[40]

- Suppressed anger – the frequency with which angry feelings are experienced but not expressed.

- Low self-esteem – lack of self-love stems from not forgiving yourself.

- Bitterness – you will feel anger, disappointment, and resentment at being treated unfairly.

- Risk of higher blood pressure.

- An increased risk of heart disease.

---

[40] https://www.counselling-directory.org.uk/memberarticles/unforgiveness-and-your-health

Not forgiving also gives the Devil the legal right to torment you. Matthew 18:23-35 tells us that if we do not forgive people, we get turned over to the torturers:

23"Therefore, the kingdom of heaven is like a king who wanted to settle accounts with his servants. 24As he began the settlement, a man who owed him ten thousand bags of gold was brought to him. 25Since he was not able to pay, the master ordered that he and his wife and his children and all that he had be sold to repay the debt.

26"At this the servant fell on his knees before him. 'Be patient with me,' he begged, 'and I will pay back everything.' 27The servant's master took pity on him, canceled the debt and let him go.

28"But when that servant went out, he found one of his fellow servants who owed him a hundred silver coins. He grabbed him and began to choke him. 'Pay back what you owe me!' he demanded.

29"His fellow servant fell to his knees and begged him, 'Be patient with me, and I will pay it back.'

30"But he refused. Instead, he went off and had the man thrown into prison until he could pay the debt. 31When the other servants saw what had happened, they were outraged and went and told their master everything that had happened.

32"Then the master called the servant in. 'You wicked servant,' he said, 'I canceled all that debt of yours because you begged me to. 33Shouldn't you have had mercy on your fellow servant just as I had on you?' 34In anger his master handed him over to the jailers to be tortured, until he should pay back all he owed.

35"This is how my heavenly Father will treat each of you unless you forgive your brother or sister from your heart."

I don't know about you, but I don't want any torturer to touch me again!

Forgiveness will bring freedom and will affect your mind, body, and spirit.

Forgiveness is not saying that what you did or what was done to you is okay. It is simply releasing the bitterness and resentment in your heart toward yourself or someone else.

When you forgive, you not only are let out of a spiritual prison, but you are given the ability to walk in the freedom you desire—to move forward toward your healing. You cannot move forward if you continue to harbor the wrongs you perpetrated against yourself or others.

Forgive and watch what happens— you will see you now have the ability to create a beautiful beam of light that can pierce the dark in even the stormiest of weather.

5. REPLACEMENT

The final step in the purification process involves replacing your negative self-talk, false accusations, and lies with truth. This allows the impurities to be extracted.

During this step, I recommend taking out a pen and a blank piece of paper and finding a quiet place. For your convenience, I have included a few blank pages at the end of this chapter for you to write notes. On one side of the page, write down all the negative qualities you see about yourself or what others have told you. Make a list down the page. Keep writing until you have exhausted yourself. You may write down words like:

"Failure"

"Worthless"

and

"Guilty"

Keep in mind that the act of writing will not automatically change your circumstances, but it may assist you in reaching a mindset shift, which is the goal.

You define yourself by these words through your broken lens.

What God sees, however, is different. He sees the truth.

Instead of failure, He sees victory.

Instead of worthlessness, He sees value.

Where you see a guilty man or woman, He sees someone who is pardoned.

He sees the opposite of what we see because He can see clearly.

Now, replace each word you have written by writing next to it a word that means the opposite. Even better, find scripture out of the Bible that shows you who you are.

For example:

You are not a failure. Instead, God says you are a conqueror.

> *"Yet in all these things we are more than conquerors through Him who loved us." (Romans 8:37)*

You are not worthless. God says you are fearfully and wonderfully made.

> *"For you created my inmost being; you knit me together in my mother's womb. I praise you because I am fearfully and wonderfully made; your works are wonderful, I know that full well." (Psalm 139:13-14)*

You are not guilty. God says you are forgiven.

> *"If we confess our sins, He is faithful and just and will forgive us our sins and purify us from all unrighteousness."* (1 John 1:9)

Read these scriptures or affirmations until you believe what they say about you! It might take hours, days, or months but hang in there.

Sometimes we are so tangled up in the lies about who we are that it could take longer than we'd hoped to finish this step—to break agreement with the Devil and align your beliefs with Heaven's thoughts of you. If you find yourself still dealing with feelings of worthlessness after this exercise—continue doing the action of declaring the truths and allowing them to wash over you.

Every day.

Write down the truth about yourself on a notecard and tape it to the mirror in the bathroom if you have to. Put it on your computer at the office. Wherever you may see it, let it be a reminder.

Because one day, those words will sink in.

One day you will believe them.

One day, the lies will wash away.

Once you have gone through this last purification step, you will have clarity as well as the ability to see and be seen differently.

You will see the world through a different lens.

You will see yourself through a different lens.

**When you replace the lies with the truth about who you are—
that you are brave, courageous, more than a conqueror,
and so on—the result is a mindset shift.**

When this takes place, you become a prism. Clear, beautiful, and sustaining, carrying power and the ability to allow light to pass through you and out into the darkness of night.

HOW I BECAME A PRISM

Becoming a prism is not easy. You will be purified by fire to become the pristine, sustainable, beautiful creation you were designed to be. In this process, impurities are melted away. While the process may not be comfortable at times, the result brings such beauty to your mind, body, and spirit!

To become a prism, you must go through the Five Purification Steps I mentioned previously. To keep these fresh in your mind, they are:

1. **Humility**
2. **Confession**
3. **Repentance**
4. **Forgiveness**
5. **Replacement**

It bears repeating that if you are postured in humility, confess your sins or wrongdoings, repent, forgive yourself and/or others, and replace the lies about who you think you are with the truth of who God says you are, then you will become a prism.

I did not become one overnight. It was a process, and I want to tell you about it.

1. HUMILITY

Merriam-Webster defines humility as "freedom from pride."[41] With humility, there is a laying down of self. My problem initially was there was no laying down—I would not sit still long enough to do that because I was too busy hating myself. Maybe deep down, I knew that if I sat quietly long enough, I would begin a healing journey. But pride didn't want that. My heart needed to remain cold.

I became disinterested in going to church—partly because I knew God could bring warmth to my heart again, but I did not want it. I felt that with a cold heart, I could be numb to the pain. A heart of stone doesn't hurt, so that's what I desired.

After a time, however, I began going to church again. My husband and I would sit toward the back, but at least we were there. During the worship songs, all I could do was sit or stand. But I was still.

It was a forced stillness, but one of the best kinds.

This was when music and words would wash over me. Most of the time, I cried, with my heart hurting… or maybe it was warmth starting to seep in.

Over time, I could feel my heart of stone become flesh. And I knew what God had done, just as He said in His Word in Ezekiel 36:26, "I will give you a new heart and put a new spirit in you; I will remove from you your heart of stone and give you a heart of flesh."

In the beginning, sitting in stillness during worship allowed me the opportunity to posture my heart the way I should. This is not the only place you can posture your heart. That's just the way it was for me.

---

[41] https://www.merriam-webster.com/dictionary/humility

As I said earlier, the way up is down.

Part of humbling myself lies in the way I would be seen.

My pride didn't want me to be seen.

Not for who I was.

That is why it took so long for me to surrender.

I didn't want the entire world to know about my failures. I didn't want my peers, family, or friends to know what I had done. I didn't want them to see me differently.

Pride couldn't look in the mirror to see the truth—fearing what it would see.

But I became weary in that game.

Eventually, I had to surrender my will to God's.

I had to go low, sitting with arms open, saying, "Here I am."

By going low, submerging myself in humility, and surrendering my heart, I freed myself from the ugliness of pride.

2. CONFESSION

Whew, this was hard. Audibly confessing my sins meant I had to look at what I had done, and all that took place afterward again, but more deeply. This was a DVD video that I had labeled "X" in dark red ink and placed in a box in the basement of my life, never to pull out again. Confession meant I had to feel, and I didn't want to do that, either. True confession is more than words coming out of your mouth. There is a heart-mouth connection, where the words you speak are an overflow of your heart. Your heart must be involved if you are to have true confession.

Confession also meant acknowledging that I wasn't perfect. Not only that, but I was nowhere near the mark. Of course, I knew that, but acknowledging it somehow made it more real! I still wanted to see myself the way I used to be, and I thought I couldn't if I examined the contents of the video that had been sitting in the box collecting dust.

Humility paved the way for me to confess without trying to justify what I had done or blame someone else.

Before humility entered, my words were just words.

I do want to make a distinction here.

On the day my professor called me into her office, I immediately confessed to the honor code violation. Although, I could barely look at her when I spoke.

I wanted to make things right again. There was nothing I could do to change things, but I vowed to redeem myself in my professor's eyes and in my own.

I confessed. I took responsibility.

My heart was in it.

Confession wasn't so easy with my marriage violation—with my infidelity.

At first.

My ex-husband confronted me with questions because he had become suspicious.

I admitted what I had done, but my heart was not in it.

I was full of hate.

Hate turns the heart cold.

A cold-hearted confession does not lead to purification.

When pride still has a stronghold, when you speak, you won't be any closer to moving through the doorway to cleansing. What you speak will only be words.

The kind of confession that moves you closer to becoming a prism is the kind where your heart *is* in it!

And this didn't happen until something happened to my heart.

Until the warmth entered when God took my heart of stone and made it flesh.

Notice He made it flesh. I did not.

When my heart was made flesh, I could confess with my words and heart connected.

I could walk through the doorway to my cleansing, actually believing that my sins could be made white as snow.

3. REPENTANCE

There is a difference between remorse and repentance. Remorse involves feeling sadness and being sorry for something you have done. Repentance, however, involves a complete heart reconstruction and change in direction. A light switch turned on when I was in full repentance.

2 Corinthians 7:10 says, "For godly sorrow produces repentance leading to salvation, not to be regretted; but the sorrow of the world produces death." Godly sorrow is based on the belief that a behavior you are committing or have committed is wrong and should be stopped. It's not

just feeling sorry for it. Out of Godly sorrow, repentance is birthed because it produces a change in one's behavior and direction. It is not a temporary thing but causes an actual change in a person.

To continue on my journey to becoming a prism, I had to be fully repentant! Owning my sin meant making no excuses or justifications and making the full resolve never to go that way again. With my law school honor code violation, I repented immediately, but it took longer for my marriage violation. I hate admitting that, but it's true. I was stuck in Remorseville longer than I'd like to admit. But once I was there, a shift came over my mind and spirit. With Godly sorrow, I understood that my life was not over. The change in my direction caused me to see that there is life after the valley of death. I understood that my sin didn't mean I had to live in the darkness of the valley continually. There was a way out. There was a way up. I just had to walk in a different direction to get there.

4. FORGIVENESS

This was the hardest thing for me to do. More than forgiving others, I had a very difficult time forgiving myself. In fact, I told myself on a loop in my brain, "I will *never* forgive myself!" And I meant it. I didn't want to give myself that grace because I felt I didn't deserve it. I had committed such monumental failures, and deep down, it seemed like I didn't have a right to be forgiven.

Even if someone had told me at the time (and they probably did) that God had forgiven me, it didn't make it any easier for me to forgive myself.

I learned, though, that unforgiveness kept me in prison. It was a place I didn't want to be, even if I felt I deserved the torture. The ungodly thoughts about myself, others' harsh words spoken over me, and the words I spoke over myself all kept me in continual torment.

How did I come to forgive myself then?

It was a process and one that began with a dream.

In this dream, I was with a woman whose children I babysat when I was in high school.

Cindy.

We were standing in her kitchen. She was wearing all white clothes; I remember she looked so peaceful. She delivered some instructions to me, although I forgot the words she spoke when I woke. I also remember feeling surprised that I would be given a dream about her.

A dear friend of mine had a dream with her in it around the same time, and in that dream, she and Cindy were both standing outside near a fence. When my friend walked up to her, Cindy said something to her about me. Again, I can't remember the exact words. My friend relayed her dream to me, and it served as confirmation that this was a message from Heaven.

I needed to meet with Cindy.

As it turns out, she owns a physical therapy company in town. I found her number, and we connected. I had no idea of the depth of her spiritual gifting or of her involvement in helping other people heal through a ministry called Restoring the Foundations (RTF). Before I moved forward with a personal ministry session, I was invited to join a Bible study at Cindy's house. In my adult life, the idea of Bible studies did not interest me—something was off-putting about the idea. Most likely because I didn't have the right mindset. These people would want us to open up and talk about personal hurts, habits, and hang-ups in our lives, and I wanted to keep all of that to myself. Plus, I didn't know exactly what to expect. Would we be assigned reading and meet to talk about it like a book club? After decades of school, I was done with homework and assignments.

Despite my assumptions, when Cindy invited me to her house, I accepted her invitation. I had also been baptized in the Holy Spirit recently—and had had some incredible encounters with God, experiencing the supernatural in ways I never had before, including an enhanced dream life.

I was listening and desired to be obedient to what I believed God wanted me to do. It seemed by the signs and messages I had been given that He wanted me in Cindy's company.

He was ripening me for the perfect time for picking.

As I continued in her company, she mentioned RTF—in fact, several women ministers from this organization were in our Bible study. This group was different. They spoke about Jesus more deeply.

It didn't take me long to sign up for a healing and deliverance ministry session with Cindy. She flew a ministry partner in from Texas for the appointment. I'll save the details of this session for another day, but I can relay that it was extremely powerful. One thing I did during my time with these ladies was to forgive other people and myself. I also broke alignment with the Devil and realigned my thoughts with Heaven's thoughts of myself. It was truly a time of healing and deliverance. For the first time in a long time, I allowed the Holy Spirit to minister to me. I allowed God to love me.

I allowed myself to love me.

Forgiveness played a key role in all of this—it allowed love to break through.

5. REPLACEMENT

The more I associated myself with the people of God, attended church regularly, and renewed my mind while reading God's Word and during worship, the easier it was for me to hear and believe the truth about who

I really am. I had to replace the false ideologies, negative self-talk, and word curses spoken over me with thoughts of Heaven.

By aligning my mind with who God's Word says I am, I could see and be seen clearly for the first time in a long time.

We are born in sin. Unless we renew our minds constantly, continuing to align with Heaven, we will not truly live in the light of the truth of who we are.

The truth is that you cannot truly replace your negative self-talk and false thoughts unless you love yourself.

Love is the greatest commandment.

When I replaced the lies with truth, my perspective changed, and I saw through a different lens.

**I became a prism, allowing light to pass
through me and out into my night.**

Now, I want to let you know that it took time for me to go through these steps. I did not have them in mind or written down anywhere to check off on a list when I completed them. I didn't wake up one day and say, "Today, I am going to forgive myself."

It was a process.

Before I went through RTF, I had at least knocked out humility, confession, repentance, and even forgiveness to a degree. But RTF is when I intentionally unaligned myself with Hell's thoughts of me and aligned myself with thoughts of Heaven and was delivered from the torment of demonic oppression. Once you take the first few purification steps, you will notice courage developing. That is what happened to me.

I not only realized that there was dawn after death's door but that I was made to live in victory!

You were made to live in victory, too.

Become a prism—your destiny is on the horizon of the future, waiting patiently for you to take this step.

NOTES

NOTES

NOTES

NOTES

CHAPTER 8

PIERCE THE NIGHT

"Your story will dispel the night.
Encourage those in flight to seek Harbor."

–A.C. Lalande

One day as I was pondering on ideas about this book, opening myself up to the painful memories of my past, these words dropped into my spirit like a song:

"Your story will dispel the night.
Encourage those in flight to seek Harbor."

I even heard a melody rise up inside me. This lyric played continuously in my mind until I found myself singing it!

Tears welled up within me as I thought about you.

It's a message for you.

It's for me.

It's for all of us.

Your story will pierce the night just like the light does. What the Enemy meant for evil, God will use for good.

Genesis 50:20 says, "You intended to harm me, but God intended it for good to accomplish what is now being done, the saving of many lives."

The saving of many lives! Do you see this? Your light will save. Your story will cause others to rise up and pierce the night with great force. Their eyes will see the light, giving them the courage to persevere.

Augustin Fresnel's invention saved many lives because the light emitted from the lighthouse struck through the night with such powerful vitality. His invention, his lens, and his story changed history.

Yours can, too.

There is no doubt in my mind that once you master the steps in this book, your light will pierce the night. To "pierce" means "(of a sharp pointed object) go into or through (something)."[42] The kind of light that can penetrate the night must be able to move sharply through it.

The good news for you is that at this point, there is no conjuring up light because it is a by-product of the steps you have taken. These steps will take you to Harbor.

THE STEPS TO HARBOR

When your light pierces the night, you have completed Steps 1–4 of The Lighthouse Method. This is no easy feat. As a reminder of what you have done when you reach this point, I am providing a short recap of the steps that must be taken for you to reach Harbor.

---

[42] https://www.lexico.com/en/definition/pierce

STEP 1: PREPARE TO RISE UP

Preparation begins in the mind, and you must cast the vision to see yourself in a higher place.

Then, commit to taking regular actions to stay healthy. Fill your time with exercise, prayer, Bible reading, and listening to a podcast on overcoming.

Honor your emotions so that you feel pain, grief, anger, and heartache and process them to heal. Feeling rather than suppressing feelings will put you on the fast track to healing.

Fight to reclaim your life. Swim. Rise up! Say to the darkness, "You have no hold on me!" Your past choices do not define you or dictate your future. Fix your eyes on the surface, find the resolve, and swim. You *will* breathe again.

As a last resort, borrow another's light until you are healed enough to shine again instead of sitting in isolation. Solitude is necessary in certain instances, but you cannot stay there forever.

STEP 2: BECOME A PRISM

You must become like a prism to shine again—so light cannot just shine in you but through you. Confessing your sins or wrongdoings, repenting, forgiving yourself and/or others, and replacing the lies about who you think you are with the truth of who God says you are, will enable you to become a conduit for light.

STEP 3: HAVE THE RIGHT SUPPORT SYSTEM

Your light will not shine without the proper support in your life holding you up. Choose to have people around you and accept help from Heaven. Accepting help is not weakness; it shows strength.

Find support in someone who will believe in, teach, challenge, validate, and love you.

STEP 4: LEARN HOW TO BEND YOUR LIGHT AND SHINE

Allowing yourself to be see-through enables you to be a conduit for light, which intensifies as it passes through you and out into the world.

STEP 5: FIND HARBOR AND BECOME IT

You will rise up out of the waters of depression, anxiety, and fear that have sought to take your life and courageously take your steps to shore.

THE POWER IN TRANSPARENCY

A prism is transparent, and when light encounters a prism, it passes through it. Water is also transparent—maybe not in the swamp land of Louisiana where I am from but think of a beach you've been to with white sands and turquoise water—Florida beaches, the Caribbean, an island in the Pacific or other place around the world.

Picture yourself looking at this beach from twenty thousand feet overhead. You can see where the white sands meet the bluish-green waters. You can see the sand gradually slope down further and further until there is nothing but the deep blue ocean in view. You can see marine life moving slowly beneath the waves.

You can see through the water, especially in the shallow seas.

It's mesmerizing.

Particularly on a sunny day.

What about on the stormy days? As one might expect, the transparency of water in shallow seas is always reduced in rough weather.[43] Why? Because a storm may cause sand, mud, and rocks from the ocean floor to rise and swirl, causing the water to become murky.

When a sailor would run aground off the coast in Fresnel's day, he was also in shallow seas. And, in many cases, so close to his destination.

This got me thinking of you. And me.

If transparency is reduced in shallow seas during a storm and the shore of your life symbolizes your destiny, you may have a harder time seeing when you are on the brink of a breakthrough—because, as I shared earlier, it's hardest right before you come out on the other side.

Instead of reaching a breakthrough, you might break.

What if you could detain a storm or avoid it altogether simply by being transparent? Or go through one and remain untouched in your pursuit to shore?

While you are not water or a prism, you too can be transparent.

You can be see-through.

Transparency is harder to achieve in a storm, but it is not impossible. And it's certainly not impossible after a storm when you're riding in the wake of your consequences. I became transparent by confessing and owning what I did.

I am still learning how to be transparent as I strive for transparency in all areas of my life.

---

[43] http://scmuseum.org/wp-content/uploads/2015/09/Shallow-Seas-4-6-Learning-Resource-Guide.pdf

When you are see-through, light can pass through you and out of you.

You will look different and feel lighter, having tossed your burdens down by the wayside—burdens that used to weigh you down.

There is power in allowing yourself to be see-through.

Being transparent should be your goal, whether in rough weather or not.

What Does Transparency Look Like?

There are many facets to being transparent, but the most important qualities are:

- You allow others to see inside the deepest parts of yourself.
- You are open to correction or criticism.
- You acknowledge your failures.
- You live in humility.
- You live with empathy.
- You admit when you are wrong.
- You acknowledge when you mess up, and you make it right.
- You follow through on promises.
- You can say, "I need help" when you need it.
- You are not hiding anything.
- You are not hiding from anyone.

You can tell who is living in transparency because these people look different. They reflect the beauty of a person living authentically.

They live without a covering.

In the Garden of Eden, Adam and Eve were made without a covering. They were naked when they were created! They only wore a covering made of fig leaves when they fell into sin and felt like they had to hide from God.

Transparency is always the ideal, but it's not something that happens without effort on your part. You must be willing to become it.

When you do, many things happen:

- You can detach from your ego and crisis and will want to help others.
- You become visible.
- Light can shine through you.
- You are living in honesty.
- You are honoring yourself.
- You inspire others.
- You can cast hope in another's life.

Transparency allows your intentions and motivations to be seen, making it easier for you to be seen.

Transparency allows you to transition from yourself to others.

You can circumnavigate yourself to reach the world around you when you are transparent.

The Latin prefix for "trans" is "across," "over," or "beyond." It is attached to verb roots that refer to movement or carrying from one place to another.[44] Earlier in this book, I spoke about a transformation that takes place when we allow ourselves to be transparent and purified by living in humility, confession, repentance, and forgiveness, and when we see with a fresh lens of truth. We only do this after replacing the lies about who we think we are with the truth of who God says we are. We transform because our mindset has shifted as the lens through which we view ourselves, and the world has been cleaned or replaced. We can now move across or

---

[44] https://www.wordreference.com/definition/trans

beyond ourselves to positively impact the world around us after a traumatic event or experience.

When you become transparent, you become visible.

Transparency allows your intentions and motivations lying under the surface to be seen, which in turn makes it easier for you to be seen.

You can't hide anything or pretend to be something you're not. In this place, you are unmasked. You no longer avoid problems. Instead, you have the tools to face them head-on. Because you have learned to own up to your mistakes, you will no longer feel the need to run.

When you become transparent, others can see who you are.

And don't you want to be seen? Really seen?

Most people like only to show the ideal parts of their lives—the parts they are proud of and feel like others would approve of. The minority wear their hearts on their sleeves, and only a select few see them.

Instead of letting the light into their hearts, a covering falls over them. We hide behind masks we've created because we don't want to let the world know we're insecure or unsteady. That's a lot of pressure to put on someone.

If left unnoticed and unmanaged, this mask will be handed down to our children, and they will wear it, too.

When you become transparent, light can shine through you.

Just as a transparent prism or other object allows light to shine through, your light can shine through and out of you when you are transparent. When you are transparent, you are nurturing relationships. It is not all about you anymore. Because you are outside of yourself, the light can shine through you. You can see outside yourself, and you're not blocking light from leaving, so it can reach others.

By moving your focus from yourself to others, you will find yourself wanting to be around other, similarly transparent people. This is the opposite of isolation. When you are not transparent, the Devil will tell you to be by yourself—you won't want people to know your business. Remember, we are stronger together! When you are transparent, you attract other like-minded people and can make divine connections.

When you become transparent, you are living in honesty.

Living in honesty makes you lighter because you are no longer carrying the heavy baggage that comes with wearing a false persona. You are living in integrity— doing what's right even when no one's looking. You have stepped over fear. You don't need to fulfill someone else's expectations that may not even be right.

When you are transparent, you are reaching out for help when you need it. If you are presented with a problem that you don't know the answer to, you can ask for help and know it doesn't mean you are weak. It means you are human! People appreciate it when others show their humanity.

When you become transparent, you are honoring yourself.

Your focus now turns to making healthy decisions versus desperate ones. Honor can be defined as "to respect, worship or accept someone or something."[45] The word "accept" was highlighted to me when I read the definition of *honor* and thought of the opposite scenario. Could it be that when we are not honoring ourselves, the truth is that we have not accepted ourselves for being where we are in life or who we have become? More deeply, could it be that this is because we do not love ourselves? Love takes us to the next level. When we love ourselves, we accept ourselves and, in

---

[45] https://www.yourdictionary.com/honor

turn, honor ourselves. In this way, being transparent means that you are being led with love.

When you become transparent, you inspire others.

Transparency empowers you to touch the world with strong self-confidence. This produces respect and trust, which can be built or, in some cases, rebuilt. Your transparency touches the world around you. While you will notice a change in yourself, your transparency will birth the desire for others to be transparent as well. Sometimes it can be taught, but it is often caught (it can happen by association or by being around someone who has decided to live transparently). Your choice to be transparent will be just the thing someone else needs to give themselves permission to do the same.

You can cast hope into another's life.

When light passes through a prism, rainbows are created. This phenomenon is possible because of the transparency of the prism. When light passes through a prism, it is separated into beautiful colors of red, orange, yellow, green, blue, indigo, and violet. There are actually close to one million colors contained in a rainbow, but these seven colors are the only ones distinguishable to the human eye.[46]

A rainbow has traditionally been known as a symbol of hope. It also serves as a reminder of God's faithfulness and mercy. We are reminded that even though we may experience great trials in this life, God will remain faithful and good. A rainbow also serves as a sign of God's covenant with man that He would never destroy life with flood waters again.

Genesis 9:13-15 says, "I have set my rainbow in the clouds, and it will be the sign of the covenant between me and the earth. Whenever I bring

---

[46] https://www.christianity.com/wiki/bible/what-is-the-meaning-of-the-rainbow-in-the-bible.html

clouds over the earth, and the rainbow appears in the clouds, I will remember my covenant between you and me and all living creatures of every kind. Never again will the waters become a flood to destroy all life."

Rainbows bring hope. If a prism was not see-through, a rainbow could not be cast. When you are transparent, you can cast hope into another's life. Just like a prism can cast rainbows on a wall (or a floor or a ceiling or just about anything), you have the same ability to cast hope because of the choice you are making to be see-through, unmasked, and vulnerable in your life and relationships.

Where Transparency Takes Place

This is an inside job.

In a lighthouse, transparent prisms and transparency happen on the inside.

If you recall from my mini physics lesson earlier in this book, the interface is the meeting place where light encounters a different medium than the one through which it has been traveling. Before light hits a prism, the medium is air. The surface of the prism is the meeting place where light encounters a different medium. If the interface were not transparent, the light would not have the ability to pass through it. However, because of the transparency of the glass that makes up the prism, the light rays can unify and go in the same direction.

They can become visible from the outside.

The bending of light and the change in the direction of light happens at the interface.

Have you noticed how close interface sounds to inner face?

I don't think it's a coincidence.

Your inner face must be see-through for your light to pierce the night. Just as the interface in the Fresnel Lens must also be transparent. Do you see the connection?

What is your inner face?

In Ephesians 1:18, Paul encourages us by saying, "I pray that the eyes of your heart may be enlightened in order that you may know the hope to which He has called you, the riches of His glorious inheritance in His holy people. Another translation (Ephesians 1:18, New Living Translation) says, "I pray that your hearts will be flooded with light so that you can understand the confident hope He has given to those He called—His holy people who are His rich and glorious inheritance."

When Paul refers to "the eyes of your heart," these are your spiritual eyes.

The eyes of your heart must be illuminated.

The only way illumination occurs is if your inner face is transparent.

Transparency is vital if you want your light to pierce the night. Your choice to do this will give another the opportunity to see your light and be saved.

Your Walk to Shore

Steps 1-4 of The Lighthouse Method are so powerful. When you complete *Step 4: Bend Your Light and Shine*, you will be far from where you started.

Here, you have faced your fears, found your footing, and taken courageous steps forward to shore.

Steps that take you to Harbor.

HARBOR

I see you.

You are the one whose feet are planted firmly on the shore.

Barefoot.

Free.

You look down and feel the sand glide between your toes.

It is early morning.

The sun has just begun peeking over the horizon, casting warmth into the sky.

The sand is cool under your feet—you know it won't be long before the sun heats the sand under them.

It is quiet.

Down the beach, a man is setting up his fishing line. You remember you used to fish with your daddy.

As you look down, you see a sliver of light shine on your leg.

Light.

You look back up and see that the sun has made its way to the shore, too.

You notice movement in the water and watch as the waves bring a fragmented seashell onto the sand from the sea.

You walk over to it and pick it up with your right hand. The shell is white and pink, with pieces of purple.

Beveled and rough.

Fragile.

You turn the shell over, and a shard breaks off in your hand.

Your mind drifts back to the days when you were broken.

To the days when you were a captive, huddled in the shadowed corner of the dingy, prison-like room you chose to live in.

Wallowing in the darkness.

Afraid and defeated, fearing you may completely break in the process if you attempt to stand up.

You felt that if you remained hidden, maybe what happened would remain hidden too.

Light? You'd say, *There's no light here.*

You spoke words of hopelessness.

You smelled of must and stagnancy, wearing the wounds of your past as armor. You thought it would protect you.

You were dressed that way for so long that you thought it was normal.

But there was nothing normal about it.

You stayed there for so long that your eyes adjusted to the dark.

But you could not see clearly.

You really could not see at all.

You were broken.

But you didn't stay that way.

You have prevailed.

You have risen above.

You have come back to life!

All the painful experiences you have endured are now fading into dust. You no longer cringe when you think of that time, for God intended it for good to accomplish what is now being done....

You walk to the edge of the water, crouch down and place the fragmented seashell into the sea.

It drifts away, as do the memories of who you once were.

You stand and breathe in the truth of who and where you are.

Where you once were lost, you are now found.

Where you once lived with hopelessness, you are now filled with peace.

Where fear used to rule, courage now reigns.

You are not the same person you used to be.

Something inside you makes you turn around, and your eyes fall on the beautiful lighthouse resting 30 feet behind you.

You turn your head in wonder at its beauty and strength, feeling an instant connection to this wooden kindred spirit.

A knowing stirs inside.

And you realize your purpose.

You are a lighthouse.

You have been refined and purified.

You have risen and taken your place.

Now it is your turn to look up and look out.

To find another lost mariner and guide them

Home.

You open your mouth and begin to sing while the notes fly across the salty air.

Drifting effortlessly with purpose

As they make their way to the person who needs to hear them.

The song you sing is your story.

The dawn to someone else's night.

A hope that can only be found in the telling.

And in the telling...

Your story will dispel the night.

Encourage those in flight

To seek Harbor.

ACKNOWLEDGMENTS

I could not have completed this book without the continual support and vision of my editor and book coach, Hilary Jastram. She taught me many things—including the value of an outline and the value of your voice. Thank you also to Heather Mize for being the final set of editing eyes to rest on this book before it was published.

To Michelle Kulp, my publisher, who has been with me since day one of this book writing journey, it feels good to be off your "straggler" list finally!

To my devoted and loving husband, Dwayne, my deepest gratitude. You encouraged me to continue in this endeavor, even on the nights when I was burning the midnight oil, and you wanted to sleep. You show me what true love is.

To my daughters, when I became a mother, I knew the Father's love for me. Out of this love, a desire to pick up my dusty pen was revived. You sparked the light that now burns in me to continue touching the human spirit with my words.

Mom, Dad, and my dear family, thank you for believing in me. You always have. You have always believed in my gift. Thank you for being my constant companions and a shoulder to hug, laugh, or cry on all the days of my life.

To L.M. Montgomery, author of Anne of Green Gables, you are the reason I first fell in love with the written word. Many thanks.

Above all, to my Heavenly Father, the redeemer of my soul and story, thank you for rescuing me.

ABOUT THE AUTHOR

Angela is a real estate attorney and the owner of Lalande Title, a real estate closing company offering home buyers, realtors, lenders, and builders title insurance, escrow, and closing services for residential and commercial properties. Her main mission is to make the closing process as smooth as possible for everyone involved in a real estate transaction.

You can connect with Angela at www.LalandeTitle.com.

Social Media:

Facebook: Facebook.com/AngelaCLalande

Facebook Business page: Facebook.com/LalandeTitle

Instagram: Instagram.com/aclalande

Instagram Business page: Instagram.com/lalandetitle

DISCLAIMER

This is a work of creative non-fiction. The author has made every effort to share true and accurate recollections. Some events, conversations, and situations have been dramatized or condensed. Any advice or recommendations in this book should not be taken as legal advice. While all the stories in this book are true, some names and identifying details have been changed to protect the privacy of the people involved. Any content provided in this book should not be taken as legal advice. Finally, although this book may be construed as a self-help book, the author is not responsible for other people's results or lack thereof.

www.ingramcontent.com/pod-product-compliance
Lightning Source LLC
Chambersburg PA
CBHW060525130626
46553CB00002B/649